英訳付き
日本折り紙帖

Origami Booklet

Japan's Traditional Culture

監修／小林一夫

Editorial Supervisor

Kazuo Kobayashi

はじめに

折り紙で日本の文化にふれる

　日本の折り紙は、はるか昔の神事にルーツを持ち、数百年の歴史を経て、庶民の手軽な遊びへと発展してきました。いまでは ORIGAMI は、創造性豊かな遊戯として世界中で親しまれ、国境も民族も超えたコミュニケーション・ツールとなっています。

　この本では、日本の代表的折り紙を通して、海外の方にも日本の四季や伝統文化を感じてもらえるように工夫しました。折り鶴で新年を祝う正月にはじまり、節分、ひな祭り、端午の節句などの季節の行事、また、着物、富士山、相撲、桜、侍など日本を象徴するものから、民話や伝説でなじみの深い動物など、まさに「日本」を感じていただける作品を集めています。その作品に豊かな表情を加えるのが、本書に収めた江戸千代紙の美しい伝統文様です。

　折り紙は脳に活発な刺激を与え、創造性・ひらめき・認識力の向上につながり、子どもから年配者まであらゆる世代が楽しめる遊びです。本書の折り紙を作りながら、季節を楽しみ、文化や伝統を大切にする日本人の心を、広く海外の方にも感じていただければ幸いです。旅行者のおみやげとしても喜ばれると思います。

お茶の水 おりがみ会館館長　小林一夫

Introduction

Experience Japanese Culture through Origami

Origami in Japan is thought to have roots in ancient Shinto rituals, gradually becoming a pastime of the common folk over several hundreds of years. Origami is now popular all over the world as a creative activity, becoming a communication tool that bridges borders and connects cultures.

In this book, we aim to bring Japan's traditional culture and deep appreciation of the different seasons to a global audience. Starting with the Crane to celebrate the New Year, we then move on to origami seen at seasonal events such as *Setsubun* (a celebration of the end of winter) in February, the *Hinamatsuri* Girls' Festival in March, and the Boys' Festival in May. Next, we present origami models of well known symbols of Japan such as the Kimono, Mount Fuji, Sumo Wrestlers, Cherry Blossoms, Samurai and more, followed by animals that often appear in Japanese folklore and legends. Through this collection you will feel the true spirit of Japan, with the beauty of traditional Edo Chiyogami patterns adding an additional layer of rich expression.

Making origami is a stimulating activity that can be enjoyed by people of all ages, from children to the elderly, and leads to improved creativity, awareness and cognitive function. When creating the origami in this book, we hope people around the world will appreciate the seasons, culture and traditions that Japanese people value. This book will also make a memorable gift for visitors to Japan!

K. Kobayashi

Kazuo Kobayashi
The Director of the Ochanomizu Origami Kaikan

Contents

折り紙で日本の文化にふれる Experience Japanese Culture through Origami

日本の伝統文様について About Traditional Japanese Patterns

この本の使い方 Using This Book

この本で使う記号の意味 The Symbols Used in This Book

基本の折り方 Basic Folds

鶴
Crane

花扇面 Hana-senmen

17

祝い鶴
Celebration Crane

雲立涌 Kumo-tatewaku

19

着物
Kimono

裾波に鶴 Hem Wave and Cranes

21

富士山
Mount Fuji

波頭 Namigashira

23

相撲取り
Sumo Wrestler

芝翫縞 Shikan-jima

25

鬼
Oni

松に鶴 Pines and Cranes

27

豆入れ
Bean Holder

大納言 Dainagon

29

女雛
Mebina

道成寺 Dojoji

31

男雛
Obina

道成寺 Dojoji

33

桜
Sakura

小桜 Kozakura

35

侍
Samurai

三階松 Sangaimatsu

37

兜
Kabuto

鳳凰に桐 Houo and Paulownia

39

鯉
Koi

青海波 Seigaiha

41

蝸牛
Snail

鱗 Uroko

43

蝶
Butterfly

蝶 Cho

45

たとう
Tato Pouch

麻の葉 Asanoha

47

ぽち袋
Pochi Bag

桔梗 Kikyo

49

箸袋
Chopstick Cover

鹿の子 Kanoko

51

もみじ
Momiji

あばれ青海 Abare-seigai

53

鼠
Mouse

竹林縞 Chikurin-jima

55

雉
Pheasant

獅子毛 Shishige

57

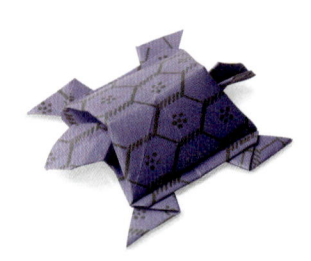

亀
Turtle

変わり亀甲 Kawari-kikko

59

雪うさぎ
Snow Rabbit

梅鉢 Umebachi

61

雪ん子
Yukinko

花菱 Hanabishi

63

折り方 How to Fold the Models

鶴 Crane ———— 65

祝い鶴 Celebration Crane ———— 67

着物 Kimono ———— 68

富士山 Mount Fuji ———— 70

相撲取り Sumo Wrestler ———— 71

鬼 Oni ———— 72

豆入れ Bean Holder ———— 73

女雛 Mebina ———— 74

男雛 Obina ———— 75

桜 Sakura ———— 76

侍 Samurai ———— 78

兜 Kabuto ———— 80

鯉 Koi ———— 81

蝸牛 Snail ———— 82

蝶 Butterfly ———— 84

たとう Tato Pouch ———— 86

ぽち袋 Pochi Bag ———— 87

箸袋 Chopstick Cover ———— 88

もみじ Momiji ———— 89

鼠 Mouse ———— 90

雉 Pheasant ———— 91

亀 Turtle ———— 92

雪うさぎ Snow Rabbit ———— 93

雪ん子 Yukinko ———— 94

日本の伝統文様について

　本書には、日本の伝統的な文様を描いた24種の千代紙が収められています。文様は自然や動植物をモチーフにしたり、単純な図形による幾何学文様や、大陸由来の文様に影響を受けたものもあります。その多くは縁起がよい「吉祥文」と呼ばれるもので、図柄には招福・長寿・繁栄・魔除けなど、さまざまな意味があります。

　日本の文様は、いまから1万年以上前の縄文時代に、土器に縄を押し当てて描かれた渦巻きや円・斜線・山形などの素朴で力強い文様にはじまります。6世紀の仏教伝来以降、大陸渡来の文化は日本に大きな影響を与え、"シルクロードの終着駅"と言われる奈良・正倉院の収蔵品には、装飾的な動植物文様や、信仰的・呪術的・説話的内容を含んだ中国古代伝統文様・西方系中国文様など多彩な文様が見られます。

　平安時代になると日本的な花鳥風月への傾倒がはじまり、鶴・松・紅葉・秋草など自然風物の散らし文様が現れます。平安の貴族文化から、鎌倉～室町～安土桃山時代には武家文化が隆盛し、文様にも写実性や象徴性が加わり、武士は不死や必勝の意味まで文様に求めました。江戸時代に入ると文様にも庶民の遊び心が加わり、ユーモアと洒落っ気のある独自の文化が華開きます。日用品をモチーフにした目出た柄や、人気の歌舞伎役者が着て大流行した着物柄も登場します。

　他国と異なる日本の特徴は「独創的で多様性をもった絵のような文様」にあります。日本人の感性と美意識が生んだ文様の世界を、どうぞ楽しんでください。

About Traditional Japanese Patterns

This book brings together 24 different *chiyogami* designs based on traditional Japanese patterns. The patterns included here are inspired by nature, flowers, plants, simple geometry and designs originating in other parts of East Asia. Many are lucky patterns that are meant to bring blessings, long life and prosperity while warding off evil.

The Japanese tradition of pattern design started more than 10,000 years ago in the Jomon period, when ropes were pressed against earthenware to make powerful rustic designs such as swirls, circles, diagonal lines and mountains. Around the 6th century Buddhism was introduced to Japan, after which East Asian culture began to influence Japan via China. The Shoso-in Treasure House in Nara, which was known as "the last stop on the Silk Road," holds artifacts that feature decorative plants and animals, as well as patterns based on ancient Chinese and Western traditions of faith, magic and legends.

Starting in the Heian period, which lasted from the 8th to 12th century, a unique Japanese style inspired by the beauty of nature began to appear, leading to patterns made of scattered natural items such as cranes, pine trees, autumn leaves and flowers. The aristocratic culture of the Heian period shifted to a flourishing samurai culture in the Kamakura, Muromachi and Azuchi-Momoyama periods that lasted through to the 16th century. New layers of realism and symbolism were added to patterns, with samurai often seeking new motifs symbolizing immortality and victory. Entering the Edo period in the 17th century, the lighthearted spirit of the common people was expressed in playful and humorous patterns. Festive motifs featuring daily items were used for special occasions, and some kimono patterns took on great popularity after famous kabuki actors wore them.

The creation of a wide variety of imaginative patterns that are almost like pictures is a unique aspect of Japanese culture. We hope you will enjoy these patterns, which have been inspired by Japan's subtle sense of beauty.

この本の使い方
Using This Book

この本の千代紙を使って、
24種類の折り紙作品がつくれます。
また、それぞれの紙の説明によって
日本の伝統文様について知ることができます。

You can make 24 origami models with
the *chiyogami* paper found in this book.
You will also learn about traditional
Japanese patterns from the explanations
that accompany each paper.

日本の文化を
楽しんでくださいね！
Dive into
Japanese culture!

1 つくりたい作品を選びます。
Choose a model you would like to make.

2 ミシン線に合わせて紙をカットします。
ミシン線にいちど折り目をつけてからカットするときれいに切り取ることができます。
Cut the paper along the perforated line.
In order to cut the paper neatly, first make a crease along the perforated line.

3 折り方の載っているページを開きます。 例）see page 66
Open to the "How to Fold" page for your model. See page 66 for an example.

4 折り図を見ながら番号順に折っていきます。折り線の位置と種類をよく見て。
完成した作品は、見本の写真と同じ位置に図柄（文様）が見えるとは限りません。
Look at the diagrams and fold in order.
Look closely at the position and types of lines.
On your completed models, the patterns will not necessarily appear
in the same position as in the sample photos.

5 できあがったら、好きな場所に飾ったり、友だちにプレゼントしましょう。
After you have finished, you can display your creation anywhere you please
or give it to a friend as a present.

6 折り方がわかったら、ほかの紙でも折ってみましょう。好きな色や柄、
いろいろな大きさの紙でつくってみると、さらに折り紙の楽しさが広がります。
Once you have got the idea, try making the model with different kinds of paper.
You can enjoy making these origami models again and again using different
sized papers of your favorite colors and designs.

この本で使う記号の意味
The Symbols Used in This Book

線の種類や矢印など、この本で使う記号の説明をします。
折り図を見るときに必要になるので記号の意味を覚えましょう。

Here we will explain the symbols used in this book, including the different folding lines and arrow marks. These symbols will help you understand the diagrams, so please remember them.

谷折り Valley fold (dashed line)

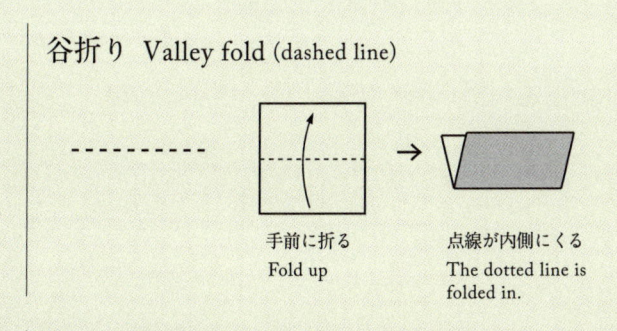

手前に折る
Fold up

点線が内側にくる
The dotted line is folded in.

折りすじをつける Make a crease (fold and unfold)

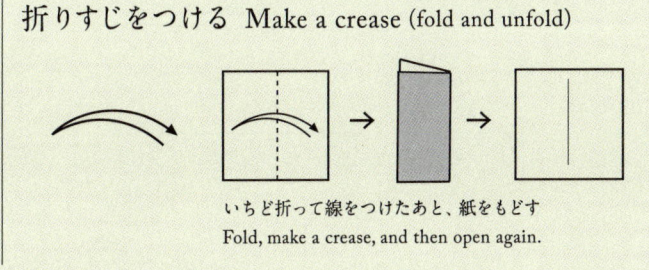

いちど折って線をつけたあと、紙をもどす
Fold, make a crease, and then open again.

山折り Mountain fold (dashed-dotted line)

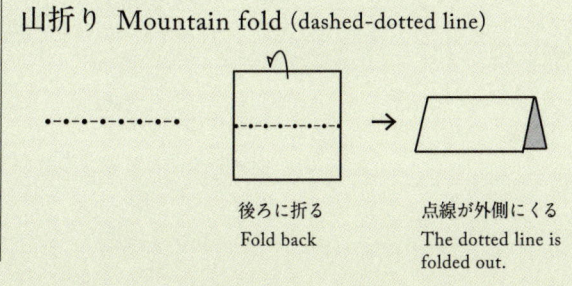

後ろに折る
Fold back

点線が外側にくる
The dotted line is folded out.

矢印の方向に折る Fold in the direction of the arrows

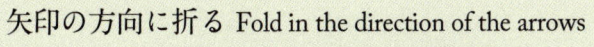
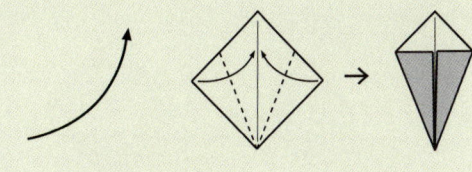

The Symbols Used in This Book

紙の向きを変える Rotate

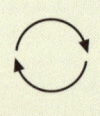 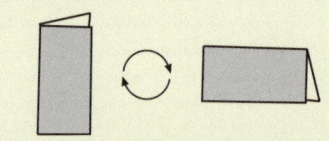

ハサミを使う Use scissors

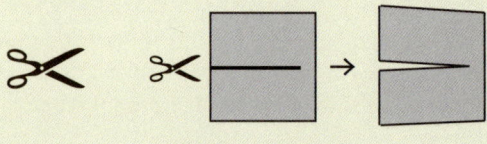

太線にそってハサミで切る
Cut along the thick line.

うらがえす Turn over

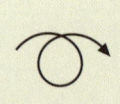 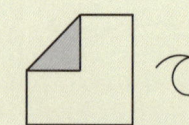 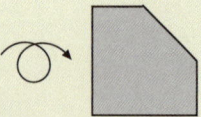

上下の位置は変えない
Do not change the orientation of the top and bottom.

紙のあいだを開く Insert fingers and open

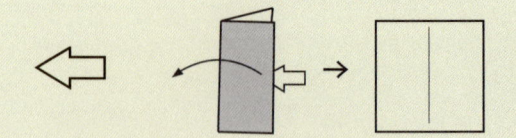

図を拡大する Enlargement

 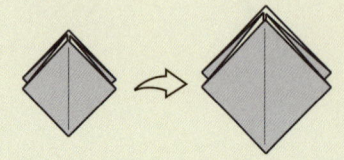

同じ幅・同じ角度 Same width, same angle

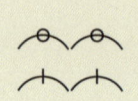 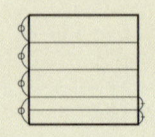 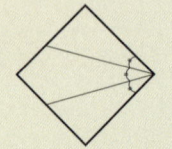

基本の折り方
Basic Folds

よく使う折り方です。とくに「四角折り」や「中わり折り」はよく使います。
These are the most common folds, especially the square base and the inside reverse fold.

四角折り Square base

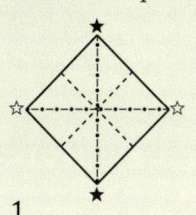 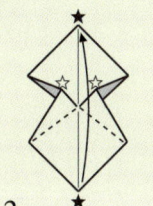 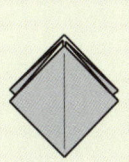

1
谷線、山線の折りすじ
をつける
Make valley and mountain
creases as shown.

2
★と★、☆と☆がつく
ようにたたむ
Fold to bring the ☆s
and ★s together.

3
できあがり
Finished!

三角折り Triangle base

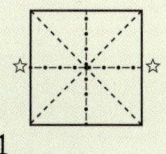 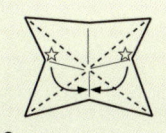 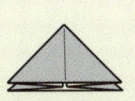

1
谷線、山線の折りすじ
をつける
Make valley and mountain
creases as shown.

2
☆と☆がつくようにた
たむ
Fold to bring the ☆s
together.

3
できあがり
Finished!

中わり折り Inside reverse fold

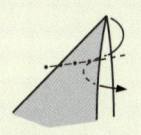 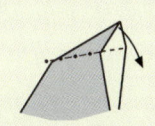 

1
折りすじをつける
Make a crease as
shown.

2
紙のさきを、内側に入
れるように折る
Push the point between
the layers and fold in.

3
できあがり
Finished!

かぶせ折り Outside reverse fold

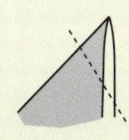 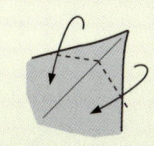 

1
折りすじをつける
Make a crease as
shown.

2
紙を上にかぶせるよう
に折る
Fold the paper over
as shown.

3
できあがり
Finished!

＊実際に折るときは折り図をよく見て、紙のうら表と上下をよく確認してはじめます。
When actually making origami, look closely at the folding diagram and carefully check the back, front, top, and bottom of the paper.

Basic Folds

かんのん折り Kannon fold

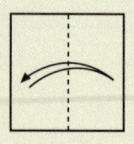 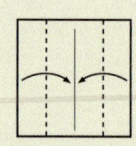 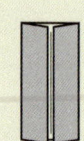

1
半分に折って折りすじ
をつける
Fold in half (make a
valley crease).

2
まん中の線まで折る
Fold both edges to
the centerline.

3
できあがり
Finished!

ざぶとん折り Blintz base

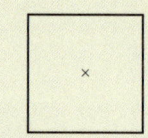 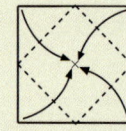 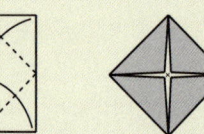

1
中心をつくる
Make a center point.

2
4つのかどを中心に向
かって折る
Fold all four corners to
the center.

3
できあがり
Finished!

※中心の印のつけ方 How to make the center point:

軽く半分に折って、まん中をおさえてもどす。別の向きから軽く半分
に折って、まん中をおさえてもどす→×印がついたところが紙の中心
Fold the paper in half lightly and pinch the center, then open. Repeat from
the opposite direction. The resulting cross mark is the center point.

段折り Pleat fold

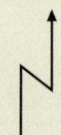 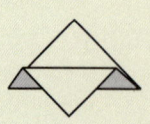

1
山折りと谷折りをして、
段をつくる
Make one mountain fold and
one valley fold, like a pleat.

2
できあがり
Finished!

凧折り Kite base

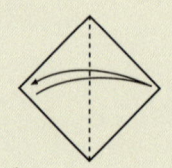 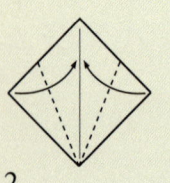

1
半分に折って折りすじ
をつける
Fold in half (make a
valley crease).

2
まん中の線まで折る
Fold both edges to
the centerline.

3
できあがり
Finished!

鶴
Crane

古来、鶴は長寿・幸福の象徴とされてきました。折り鶴は世界中で最も親しまれている折り紙で、平和や友好の印としても愛されています。

Since ancient times, the crane has been a symbol of longevity and happiness. The paper crane is famous around the world, loved everywhere as a sign of peace and friendship.

see page 65

花扇面

Hana-senmen : Flowers and Fans

流水に浮かぶ花と扇をデザインした大
変縁起のよい文様です。扇は末広がり
の形から吉祥文（縁起のよい図柄）とさ
れ、着物の柄や家紋などに広く使われ
ました。

A very lucky pattern of flowers
and folding fans floating on
running water. Upward facing open
folding fans symbolize expanding
opportunity and wealth due to their
outspread upper sides, and were
often used for kimono patterns and
family crests.

祝い鶴
Celebration Crane

正月や婚礼などのおめでたい席に
飾られる鶴です。羽が扇のように
広がるので、福を招く縁起のよい
折り紙です。

A crane that is displayed
at festive occasions such as
New Year celebrations and
weddings. Because its wings
spread like a folding fan, it is
considered to be auspicious and
invite good fortune.

see page 67

くもたてわく
雲立涌

Kumo-tatewaku

「立涌」の曲線は水蒸気の立ち昇るよ
うすを表したもの。ふくらみに雲を配
した雲立涌は、公家や皇族の装束や調
度に用いられる高貴な文様です。

The curved lines of *tatewaku*
patterns represent rising steam.
This pattern was reserved
for aristocracy, and used in
costumes and furnishings by
nobles and royalty.

着物
Kimono

着物は日本の伝統的な衣装です。季節感豊かな自然の風物やさまざまな伝統文様が、表の柄に取り入れられています。

The kimono is a traditional Japanese garment. Kimono designs often feature rich seasonal motifs inspired by nature or traditional patterns.

see page 68

裾波に鶴
<small>すそなみ</small>

Hem Wave and Cranes

鶴は長寿やめでたいことの象徴とされる吉祥文です。水辺から空に向かって飛び立つ鶴の姿は幸福への旅立ちを連想させ、婚礼衣装にも使われます。

Patterns including the crane symbolize longevity and bring luck. The crane rising from the water to the sky represents a journey to happiness and is often found on wedding kimonos.

富士山
Mount Fuji

富士は日本一標高の高い山で、そ
の美しく雄大な姿から信仰の対象
にもなってきました。日本人の心
のふるさとのような存在です。

Mount Fuji is the highest
mountain in Japan. With
its beautiful and majestic
appearance it has also become
a symbol of faith and is
considered to be the home of
the Japanese heart.

see page 70

波頭
Namigashira : Wave Head

海に囲まれた日本では、波の形まで文様の意匠に取り入れました。富士山と波の相性は、葛飾北斎の世界的に有名な浮世絵「神奈川沖浪裏」で見られるとおりです。

Japan is surrounded by the sea, inspiring artists to incorporate the shape of the wave into many designs. The affinity of Mt. Fuji and the waves is seen in artist Katsushika Hokusai's world famous *ukiyo-e* work called *The Great Wave off Kanagawa.*

相撲取り
Sumo Wrestler

相撲は日本固有の格闘技で1500
年以上の歴史があります。力士は
"まわし"という独特の帯を締めて
闘います。二つ作って闘わせる遊
びもあります。

Sumo is a unique Japanese
martial art with over 1500 years
of history. The wrestlers fight
wearing a belt called a
mawashi. Make two to play
paper sumo wrestling.

see page 71

芝翫縞
Shikan-jima

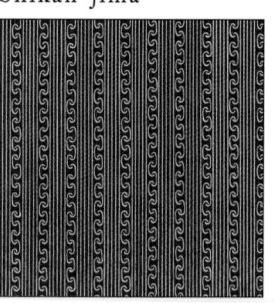

四本または五本の線と鐶つなぎが交互に並ぶ縦縞で、江戸時代に流行した歌舞伎模様の一つ。四鐶縞というべきところ、三代目中村歌右衛門の俳号「芝翫」にちなんでこの名がつきました。

A Kabuki pattern that was popular in the Edo period, alternating 4 or 5 vertical stripes with interlocked *tansu* drawer handles. The name of this pattern is *shikan-jima*, using not the kanji for *shikan* meaning "4 drawer handles," but the kanji for *shikan* used by Kabuki actor Nakamura Utaemon III as an alias.

鬼

Oni : Ogre

鬼は人間に近い姿をした想像上の怪物。昔から二月の節分には、人に災厄をもたらす邪鬼を追い払う意味で、「豆まき」をする風習があります。

The *oni* is an imaginary monster like a ogre or demon that looks nearly human. On the day of *setsubun*, a celebration of the end of winter in February, Japanese people traditionally throw beans to ward off *oni* and misfortune.

see page 72

松に鶴
Pines and Cranes

松も鶴も寿命千年といわれる縁起のよい文様なので、めでたさも倍増する図柄になっています。赤い鬼は人間の欲望や悪い心の象徴ですが、こんな文様なら人に悪さはしなくなりそうです。

Both pine trees and cranes are said to live a thousand years and bring luck. This pattern includes both of them, and brings twice the fortune. The red *oni* is a symbol of human desire and malice, but with this pattern it will be difficult for it to cause any trouble.

豆入れ
Bean Holder

節分の「豆まき」の豆を入れるのにちょうどいい箱の折り紙です。「豆まき」には煎った大豆を用い、年の数だけ食べて無病息災を祈ります。

A folded box which is just right for the bean throwing tradition of *Setsubun*. Roasted soybeans are used, and participants eat the same number of beans as their age to bring health and longevity.

see page 73

大納言
Dainagon

「大納言」とは昔の朝廷の官位で、左大臣、右大臣、内大臣に次ぐ高い位でした。花菱を草が丸く囲むこの文様は、糸を浮かせて文様を織りだす「浮線綾文」の一つで、身分の高い人だけが用いる有職文様です。

Dainagon, or great councilor, was a high official rank of the old Imperial Court, just below the left, right, and central ministers. With flowers encircled by grasses, this is one of the *fusenryo* patterns that were made in relief with raised threads, and was a professional pattern reserved for those of high rank.

女雛
Mebina : Empress Doll

女の子の成長と幸せを願う三月の「雛祭り」には、雛人形を飾ります。女雛は皇后の姿を模した人形で、古風な衣装を着ています。

Hina dolls are displayed at the *Hina-matsuri* doll festival in March, which celebrates the growth and happiness of girls. This is an origami of the *mebina* empress doll, wearing a traditional royal costume.

古式の並べ方　Ancient display position.

see page 74

道成寺
どうじょうじ

Dojoji

能楽「道成寺」や歌舞伎で着る衣装か
らきた丸紋尽くしの文様です。丸紋に
はさまざまな吉祥文が描かれ、舞台で
は魔物を鎮める人物の衣装としてよく
使われます。

A pattern of round crests from
costumes worn in the Noh play
called *Dojoji* and also in Kabuki
performances. Each of the circle
crests contain a symbol that
brings good luck. Costumes with
this pattern are often worn by
characters that tame evil spirits.

男雛

Obina : Emperor Doll

「雛祭り」に飾る天皇の姿を模した人形の折り紙です。女雛と一対で内裏雛と呼ばれ、実際の人形は衣装も細かく再現されています。

This is an origami of the *obina* emperor doll displayed during the *hina-matsuri* doll festival. It is paired with the *mebina* empress doll. The dolls and their clothing are traditionally modeled in fine detail.

see page 75

道成寺
Dojoji

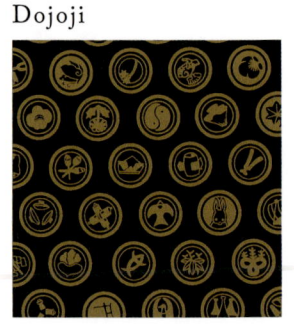

「道成寺」は、日本の伝統芸能である
能・狂言や歌舞伎の衣装に用いられる
ため「狂言家紋」と呼ばれることもあ
ります。個性豊かなさまざまな家紋を
あしらった丸紋尽くしが特徴です。

The Dojoji pattern is used for
costumes in traditional Japanese
performing arts such as Noh,
kyogen (comedic Noh interludes),
and Kabuki. It is sometimes called
kyogen-kamon, meaning "*kyogen*
family crests". Each circle in the
pattern contains an interestingly
designed family crest.

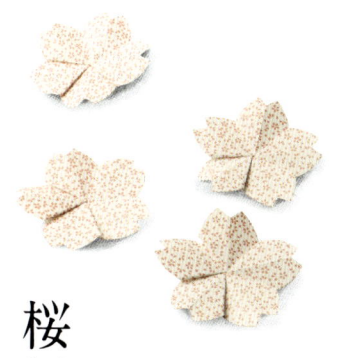

桜

Sakura : Cherry Blossoms

日本の国花で、古来、日本人に最
も愛されてきた花です。桜の開花
が春を告げ、桜の木の下で宴を催
す「花見」が各地で行われます。

The sakura is the national
flower of Japan and has been a
favorite since ancient times. The
flowering of the sakura tree
marks the arrival of spring.
Cherry blossom viewing parties
are held under sakura trees
around the country.

see page 76

小桜

Kozakura : Little Cherry Blossoms

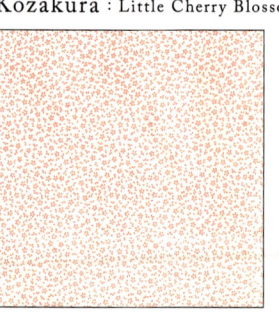

ごく小さな桜の花びらを小紋のように
ちらした文様です。それまで梅を愛好
する風習があった日本で、平安時代か
ら桜が好まれるようになり、江戸時代に
は庶民も桜を愛でるようになりました。

A pattern of very small cherry
blossom petals like small
crests. Traditionally *ume* plum
blossoms were popular, but cherry
blossoms gained a foothold in the
Heian period and then came to be
loved by commoners in the Edo
period.

侍
Samurai

侍は武芸をもって主君に仕える
人々で、江戸時代まで存在しまし
た。礼儀や格式を重んじ、非常の
際には刀や槍で戦いました。

Samurai honed battle skills to
protect local lords up until the
end of the Edo period. They
were courteous and proper,
but would fight valiantly with
swords and spears when under
attack.

see page 78

三階松

Sangaimatsu : Three Layered Pines

風雪にも耐え、四季を通じて緑を保つ
松は、長寿や清浄の意味をもつ吉祥文
で、節操を重んじる武家にも好まれま
した。日本の正月には神様の依り代と
して門松や松飾りが飾られます。

Pine trees, which withstand wind and
snow to stay green year round, represent
longevity and purity. This pattern was
popular with the samurai class, which
valued integrity, and thought to bring
good fortune. During the New Year
in Japan, pine decorations are displayed
on doorsteps to summon the gods.

兜

Kabuto ：Samurai Helmet

兜は昔、戦争のときに侍や武将が
かぶったもの。現在は、男の子の
成長と幸福を願って五月五日の
「端午の節句」に飾られます。

These helmets were worn by
samurai and warlords during
battle. These days they are
displayed on May 5 for Japan's
Boys' Festival, to celebrate the
growth and happiness of boys.

see page 80

鳳凰に桐
Houo and Paulownia

鳳凰は中国伝来の想像上の霊鳥で、桐の木に棲むと考えられていました。古来、鳳凰も桐も皇族など高貴な人々だけが使う特別な文様で、のちには将軍家が桐を家紋に使うようになりました。

The *houo* is a mythical spirit bird from China that was thought to live in a paulownia tree. In ancient times, the use of *houo* and paulownia patterns was limited to royalty and nobles. *Shogun* military rulers also used paulownia as a family crest.

鯉

Koi : Carp

鯉は日本各地の川や湖沼にすむ淡
水魚で、観賞用として錦鯉も有名
です。「端午の節句」に飾る鯉の
ぼりには、男子の出世の願いが込
められています。

Koi are freshwater fish that live
in rivers and lakes throughout
Japan, and *nishikigoi* are a
famous ornamental variety.
During the Boy's Festival
in May, koi windstreamers,
which symbolize hope for the
prosperity of boys, are displayed.

see page 81

青海波
せいがい は

Seigaiha

もとは雅楽の曲名からきた名で、海の
波のように半円形の曲線が繰り返され
る文様です。海は生命の源であり、無
限に繰り返す波のように繁栄をもたら
すとされる吉祥文です。

This pattern of semi-circles
represents waves in the sea and is
named after a popular song in the
royal court. The sea is the source
of all life, and this pattern is said
to be blessed with infinite waves of
prosperity.

かたつむり
蝸牛
Snail

春から夏に移る前に日本は「梅
雨」という雨の季節を迎えます。
雨季に見られるかたつむりは"で
んでんむし"の別名もあります。

Before moving from spring to
summer, Japan enters a rainy
season called *tsuyu*. Snails,
which can often be seen
during the rainy season, are
called either *katatsumuri* or
dendenmushi.

see page 82

うろこ
鱗
Uroko : Scales

三角形が交互に連続する文様で、古代
から世界各地で見られる意匠です。魚
や蛇の鱗に似るためにこの名がつき、
再生や魔除けの意味をもちます。歌舞
伎では蛇の化身の衣装に使われます。

Ancient designs of continuous
triangles similar to this one can be
found around the world. In Japan
it is interpreted as fish or snake
scales, symbolizing rebirth and
warding off malevolent spirits. It
is often used for snake character
costumes in Kabuki.

蝶
<ruby>蝶<rt>ちょう</rt></ruby>
Butterfly

その優美な姿から着物や洋服、装
飾品の柄によく用いられます。古
くは不死不滅の象徴として武家の
紋章にも使われました。

The graceful butterfly is often
found in kimono, clothing, and
ornament designs. In the past,
the butterfly was used in the
crests of many samurai families
as a symbol of immortality.

see pages 84

蝶

Cho : Butterfly

優美な蝶の姿は、平安時代には公家の
装束に用いる有職(ゆうそく)文様となりました。
サナギから蝶に生まれ変わる神秘性は、
不死不滅への願いから武士にも好まれ
ました。これは現代的意匠の蝶の文様
です。

Due to their great elegance, in the
Heian era butterfly patterns were
often used on the robes of nobles.
The mysterious rebirth of the
chrysalis to a butterfly made this
a popular pattern among samurai,
who desired immortality. This is a
modern butterfly design.

たとう
Tato Pouch

「たとう」は畳紙（たとうがみ）の
略で、和紙を折りたたんだものを
さします。これは中が開閉できる
ので小物入れにも使えます。

Tato is short for *tato-gami*
(folded Japanese *washi*
paper). This pouch can be used
to carry small items since it can
be opened and closed.

see page 86

麻の葉

Asanoha : Hemp Leaves

麻の葉を図案化した文様で、麻は丈夫
でまっすぐ成長することから、昔は赤
ちゃんの産着の柄によく使われました。
魔除けの意味もあり、江戸時代には庶
民の着物に大変多く用いられました。

This is a stylized pattern of hemp
leaves. In the past, it was often
used in swaddling clothes for babies
because hemp is strong and grows
straight. It was also said to ward
off evil spirits, and was common
on the kimonos of commoners in
the Edo period.

ぽち袋
Pochi Bag

心付けやおこづかいなど少額のお金を渡すときに使う袋です。ぽちには「小さい」とか「少しだけ（これっぽっち）」の意味があります。

This paper wrapping is used when giving small tips or giving children pocket money. *Pochi* means "small" or "just a little" in Japanese slang.

see page 87

桔梗
き きょう

Kikyo : Bellflower

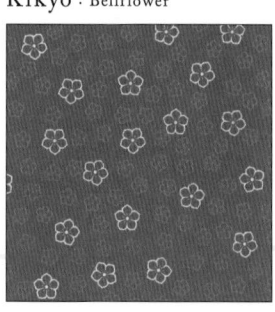

「秋の七草」の一つで、美しい紫の花をつけます。家紋にも多く用いられ、桔梗紋を用いる戦国時代の武将も多くいました。これは桔梗の花に濃淡をつけてちらした愛らしい図柄です。

Bellflowers, with their beautiful purple blooms, are one of the seven flowers that represent autumn in Japan. Many warriors in the *Sengoku* Warring States period used bellflower crests. This charming design is made up of bright bellflowers scattered on a background of faded ones.

はしぶくろ

箸袋
Chopstick Cover

使用前の箸を入れておく袋です。
日本の箸は木や竹製のものが多く、
袋に入れるのは衛生上の理由と客
へのもてなしの意味もあります。

A cover for a new set of
chopsticks. Japanese chopsticks
are often made of wood or
bamboo. Placing them in a
decorative cover not only keeps
them clean but also shows warm
hospitality.

see page 88

鹿の子
Kanoko

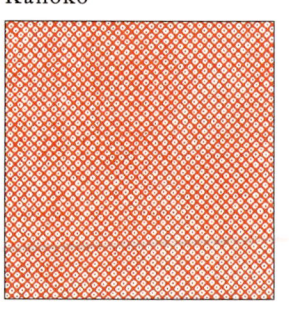

鹿の体毛の白い斑点のような細かい連続文様を「鹿の子」といいます。小さな点がすき間なく並ぶ文様で、もとは「鹿の子絞り」という大変手間のかかる染めの技法で生まれる文様です。

Continuous patterns of
fine white spots like those on
a fawn's back are called *kanoko*.
This dense pattern of small dots
is created with a delicate and
intensive tye-dyeing technique
called *kanoko shibori*.

もみじ

Momiji : Japanese Maple

日本の秋の楽しみは「紅葉狩り」
です。色づいた山や森の自然に身
をおき、赤や黄色のきれいな葉っ
ぱを持ち帰って飾ったりします。

Part of the fun of autumn in
Japan is *momiji-gari*, or hunting
for red leaves. People enjoy
going to the countryside to
view the vibrant fall colors of
the mountains and forests, and
some people like to bring home
red and yellow leaves for display.

see page 89

あばれ青海
せいがい

Abare-seigai

青海波の変形で、ところどころ荒波が
砕けている文様です。江戸の図案家の
ちょっとした遊び心が感じられます。
よく見ると、砕ける波の表現が葛飾北
斎の浮世絵の波に似ています。

A variant of the *seigaiha* blue
sea waves pattern, but with
waves breaking here and there.
Edo designers showed a sense
of playfulness in designs like
this one. If you look closely, the
breaking waves are similar to
waves in the work of the legendary
ukiyo-e artist Katsushika Hokusai.

鼠
<ruby>鼠<rt>ねずみ</rt></ruby>

Mouse

日本には自分の生まれ年を十二種の動物にあてはめる「<ruby>干支<rt>えと</rt></ruby>」という中国伝来の暦があり、その最初にくる動物がねずみです。

The mouse is the first of 12 animals in Japan's traditional *eto* calendar, which is based on the Chinese zodiac. Each year is assigned one animal, and Japanese people are aware of which animal represents their birth year.

see page 90

竹林縞

Chikurin-jima : Bamboo Forest Stripes

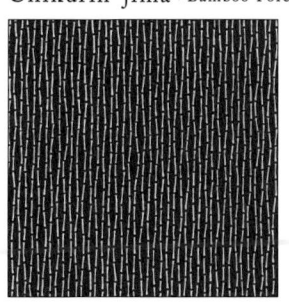

南蛮貿易によって異国風の縦縞の布地
が入ってきて以来、庶民はさまざまな
縞模様を生み出し、江戸時代には縦縞
の柄が大流行しました。これは竹林に
見立てて、ところどころ節のある縞です。

After the arrival of exotic-
style vertically striped fabrics via
the southern ports, commoners
created an abundance of new striped
patterns locally, with vertical striped
patterns booming in the Edo
period. These stripes are patterned
after a bamboo forest, with the lines
coming together here and there.

きじ
雉
Pheasant

日本の国鳥です。オスは美しく勇
敢で、メスは母性愛が強いといわ
れます。古い書物や民話にも登場
し、日本人になじみの深い鳥です。

The pheasant is the national
bird of Japan. Males are said
to be handsome and brave,
and females to show motherly
love for their young. Pheasants
appear in many old writings
and folktales, and are an easily
recognized symbol in Japan.

see page 91

獅子毛

Shishige : Chinese Lion Fur

<ruby>唐<rt>から</rt>獅<rt>じ</rt>子<rt>し</rt></ruby>の体の巻き毛を図案化した文様
です。「獅子舞」の胴体の布にも描かれ、
「<ruby>毛<rt>け</rt>卍<rt>まん</rt>文<rt>もん</rt></ruby>」ともいいます。古代、獅子
は太陽の力を宿す聖獣と考えられ、そ
の象徴的な文様です。

A pattern designed with the curly
hair of a Tang dynasty lion. It's
used for the body of the lion
costume in lion dances, and is
sometimes called *kemanmon*. It
also represents the sun, because
traditionally the lion was a sacred
beast in which the power of the
sun dwelled.

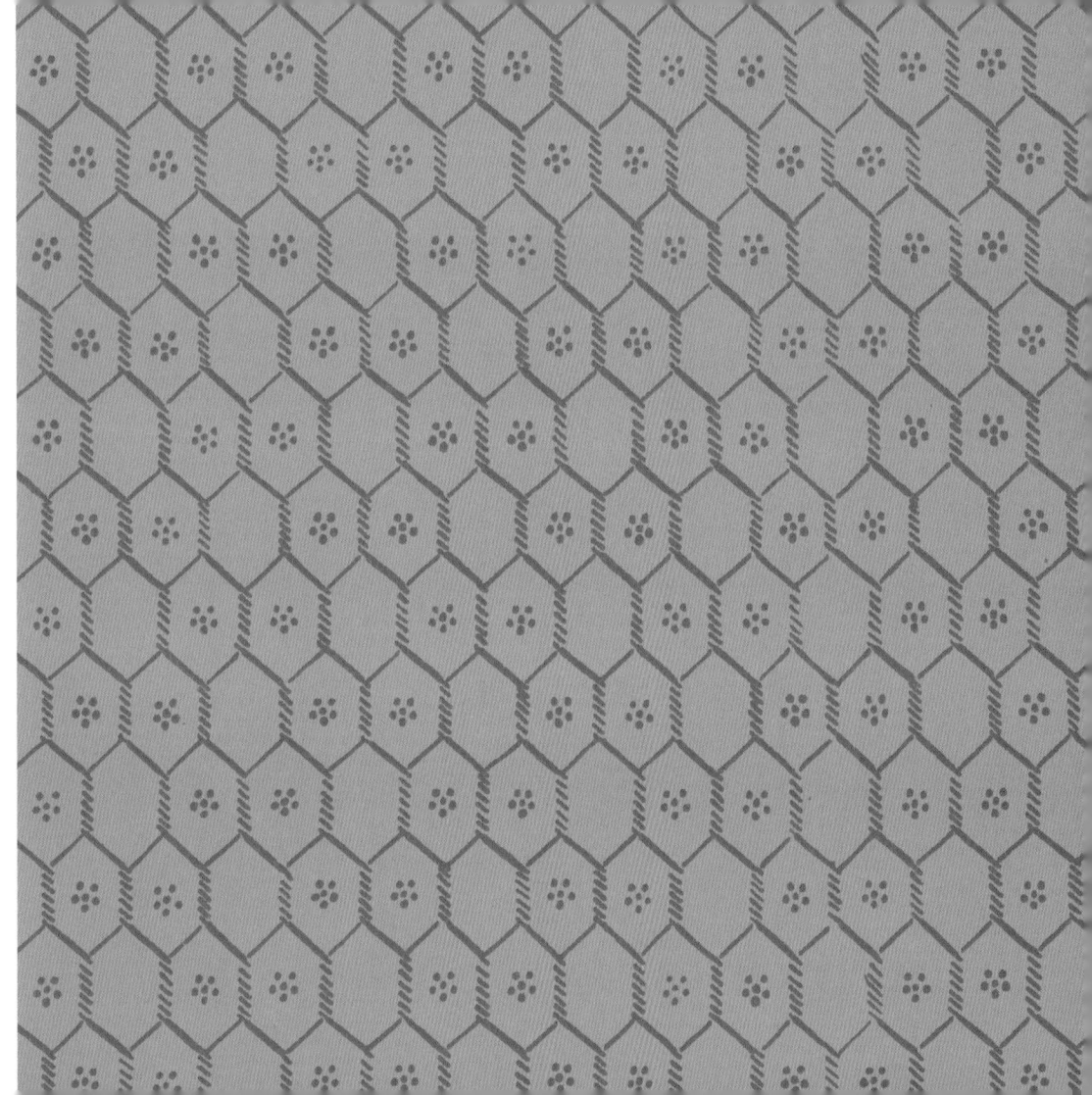

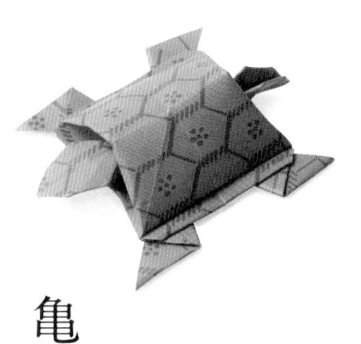

亀
Turtle

日本には古くから「鶴は千年、亀は万年」ということわざがあります。亀は鶴とともに長寿で縁起のよい動物として親しまれています。

There is an old saying in Japan that "a crane lives a thousand years, and a turtle lives ten thousand years." Turtles and cranes are much loved symbols of long life and luck.

see page 92

変わり<ruby>亀甲<rt>きっこう</rt></ruby>

Kawari-kikko : Playful Turtle Shells

六角形をつなぎ合わせた幾何学文様は
西アジアでも見られ、日本では亀の甲
羅に似ていることから亀甲の名がつき
ました。平安時代から使われる吉祥文
で、この変わり亀甲をはじめ多くのバ
リエーションがあります。

Six-sided geometric motifs are seen
across West Asia. In Japan it was
given the name *kikko*, or turtle shell,
because it resembles the back of a
turtle. The turtle shell design has
many variations, and has been used
since the Heian period as a lucky
pattern.

雪うさぎ
Snow Rabbit

雪でつくったうさぎをイメージし
た折り紙です。雪国では雪を丸く
固めて、葉っぱで耳を、赤い実で
目をつくって盆の上に飾ります。

This origami represents a rabbit
made of snow. In snowy regions
of Japan, snow rabbits are made
by using a round snow ball for a
body, then adding leaves for ears
and red fruits for eyes.

see page 93

雪ん子

Yukinko : Snow Child

綿入れを着た雪国の女の子をイ
メージした折り紙です。雪の日に
子どもの姿をした雪の精が現れる
「雪ん子伝説」もあります。

This origami is in the shape
of a girl in the snow wearing a
warm cotton-padded kimono
coat. The *yukinko* snow child
legend says a snow spirit will
appear as a child on snowy days.

see page 94

花菱

Hanabishi : Flower Chestnut

菱形の変形で、花を円形に図案化して
連続させた文様です。菱（沼や池に生
える水草）の実の形にした幾何文様は
古代から見られ、江戸時代の庶民の着
物柄としても人気がありました。

A pattern of circular flowers based
on the *hishi* water chestnut design.
Motifs of the diamond-shaped
seeds of the water chestnut, a
plant found in marshes and ponds,
have been seen in geometrical
patterns through the ages
and were popular with commoners
in the Edo period for kimonos.

鶴 Crane [see page 17]

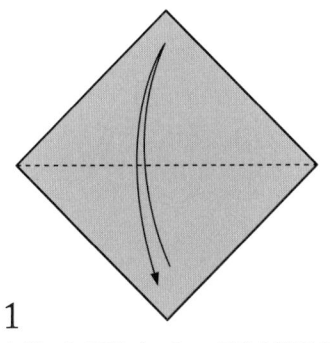

1

文様のある面を上にして、三角を横半分に折り、折りすじをつける。

Place the pattern side up.
Fold into a triangle and make a crease.

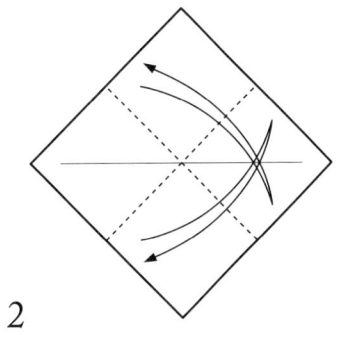

2

さらに図のように2本折りすじをつける。

Turn over and make 2 creases as shown.

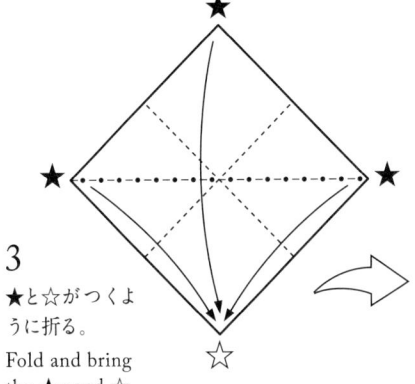

3

★と☆がつくように折る。

Fold and bring the ★s and ☆ together.

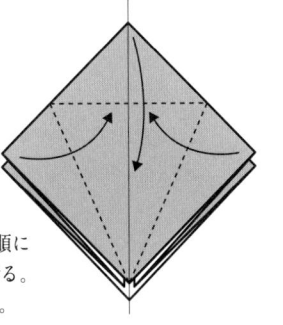

4

中心線を決めて、左右と上の順にかどが中心線上にくるように折る。うらも同様に左右のかどを折る。

Fold the sides to the center, then fold the top corner down. Fold the sides to the center on the back as well.

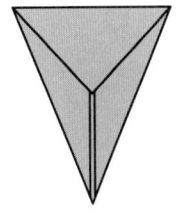

5

このように折って、4の形に戻す。

Fold like this, then return to the shape of step 4.

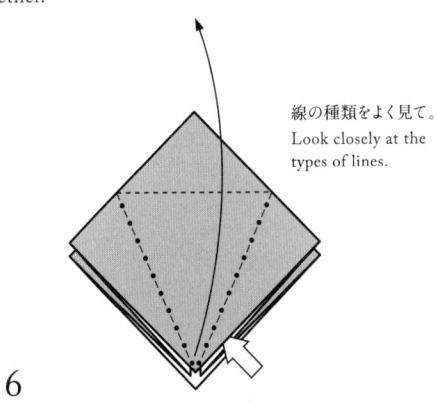

線の種類をよく見て。
Look closely at the types of lines.

6

上の1枚を開き、折りすじにそって折る。

Open the top flap and fold along the creases.

次のページへ　Continued on the next page.

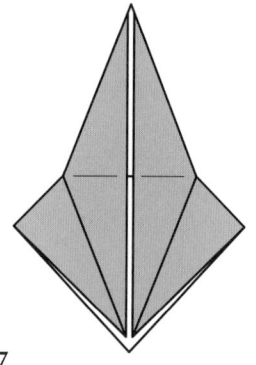

7

開いて折ったところ。うらも同じに。

It will look like this.
Repeat on the back.

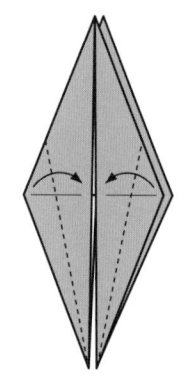

8

中心に合わせて折る。うらも同じに。

Fold the edges to the center.
Repeat on the back.

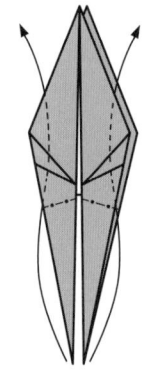

9

中わり折り（P.15）する。

Inside reverse fold (page 15).

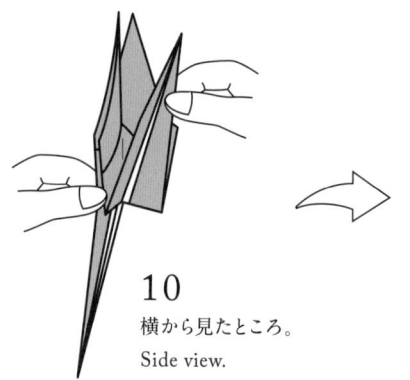

10

横から見たところ。

Side view.

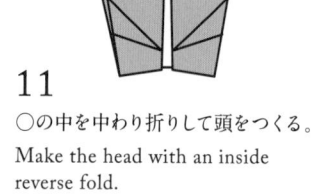

11

○の中を中わり折りして頭をつくる。

Make the head with an inside
reverse fold.

羽を広げて、
できあがり

Open the wings.
Finished!

祝い鶴 Celebration Crane [see page 19]

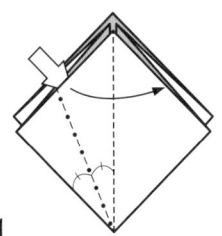

1

文様のある面を内側に四
角折り（P.15）からはじめる。
折りすじをつけて、あいだ
を開いてつぶす。

Start with the square
base (page 15), with the
patterned side facing in.
Crease and then open
and squash the left flap.

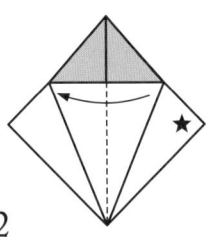

2

上の1枚を左に折る。
★も1～2と同じに折る。

Fold the top flap to the
left. Repeat 1 and 2 on
the flap marked with a ★.

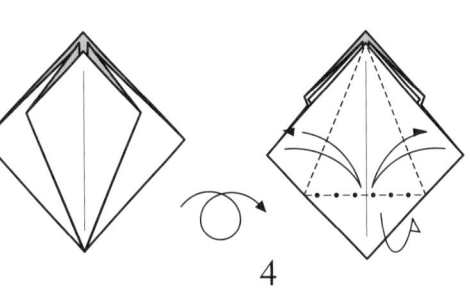

3

折ったら左右対称にする。

Arrange so it is
symmetrical
and then turn over.

4

左右に折りすじをつけてか
ら、下の部分を山折りする。

Crease both sides.
Fold up the bottom.

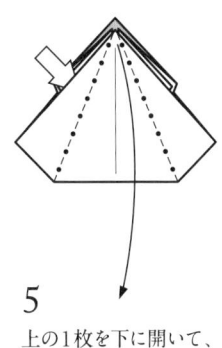

5

上の1枚を下に開いて、
たたむ。

Open the top flap and
fold down.

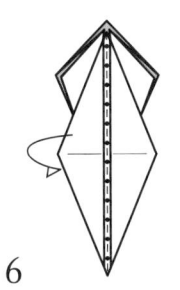

6

全体を二つ折りにする。

Fold in half.

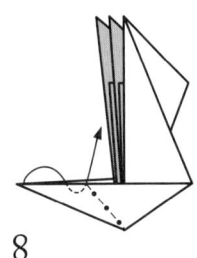

7

折りすじをつけて、かぶ
せ折り（P.15）をする。

Crease and make an
outside reverse fold
(page 15).

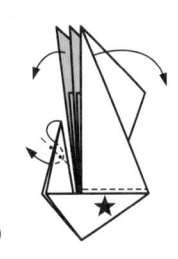

8

折りすじをつけて、中
わり折り（P.15）する。

Crease and make an
inside reverse fold
(page 15).

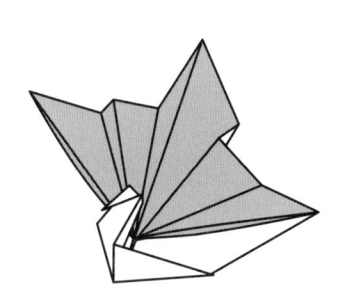

9

中わり折りで頭をつくり、
★をおさえて羽を広げる。

Make the head with an
inside reverse fold.
Open its wings while
holding at the ★.

できあがり
Finished!

着物 Kimono [see page 21] ✂

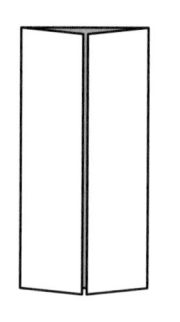

1

文様のある面を内側に、かんのん
折り（P.16）からはじめる。

Start with the kannon fold
(page16), with the patterned
side facing in.

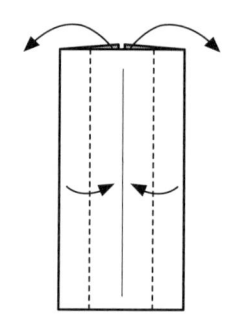 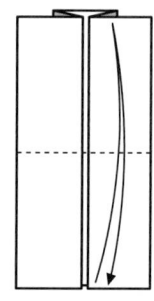

2

うら側の部分を引き出しながら、左右
をまん中の線に合わせて折る。

Allowing the back sides to flip out,
fold the edges to the centerline.

3

横半分に折りすじをつける。

Fold in half and unfold.

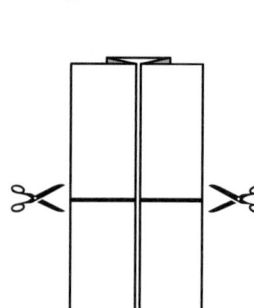 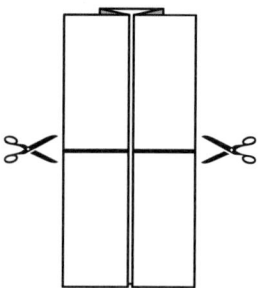

4

上の1枚に切り込みを入れる。

Cut only the top flaps as shown.

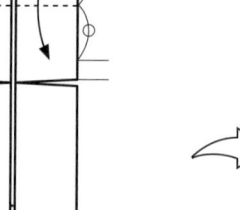 

5

切り込みの少し上まで折る。

Fold the top down to a little above the cut.

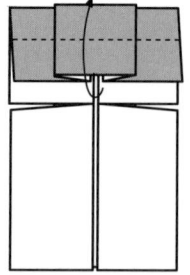

6

上端から少し上に出るように折る。

Fold back again to a little over the edge.

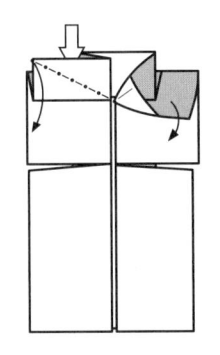

7

指を入れて上の1枚を開きながら
折りたたむ。

Insert a finger, open and squash.

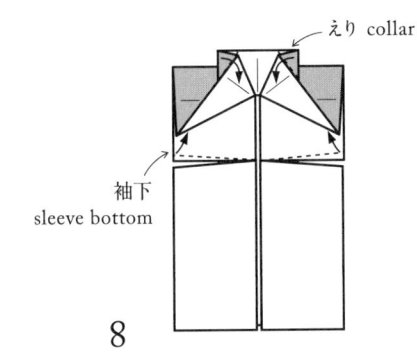

えり collar

袖下
sleeve bottom

8

えりのかどと、袖下を少し折る。

Fold down both corners of the
collar and fold up both sleeve
bottoms a little.

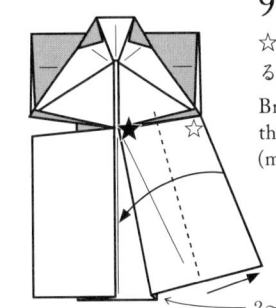

9-2

☆がまん中の線に合うように折
る（図10の形になるように）。

Bring the ☆ marked edge to
the centerline and fold
(make it look like 10 below).

2～3ミリ残す。
Leave 2 to 3 mm at
the bottom corner.

9-1

★を押さえ、下の部分を斜め
に引き出して折る。

Hold at the ★ mark,
then pull the lower flap out
diagonally.

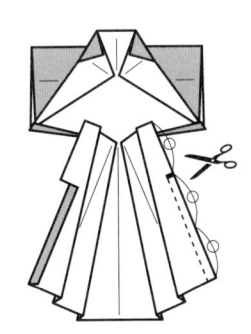

10

●が○に合うように斜めに折る。

Fold back diagonally,
so the ● meets the ○.

左側も9-1,2, 10を同様に。

Repeat steps 9-1, 9-2 and
10 on the left side.

2～3ミリ残す。
Leave 2 to 3 mm at
the bottom corner.

11

図の位置で少し切り込み
を入れ、その下を谷折りす
る（左側は折ったところ）。

Make a small cut as
shown and then valley
fold the lower edge on
each side (the left has
already been folded).

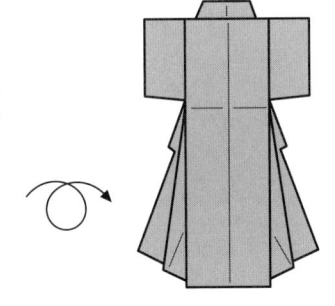

できあがり
Finished!

富士山 Mount Fuji [see page 23]

原案／渡部浩美
Draft by Hiromi Watabe

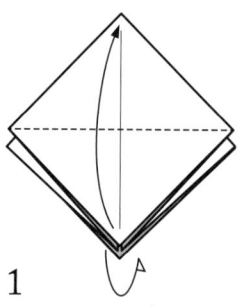

1

四角折り（P.15）からはじめて、上の1枚を谷折りする。うらも同じに。

Start with the square base (page 15) and valley fold the top flap. Turn over and repeat.

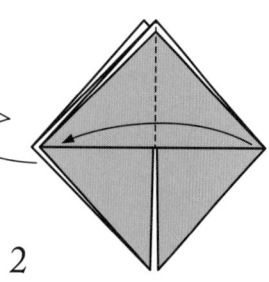

2

上の1枚を左に谷折りする。うらも同じに。

Fold the right flap to the left. Turn over and repeat.

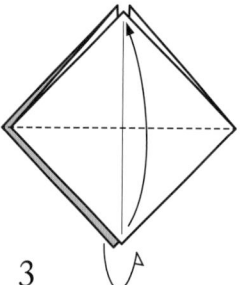

3

上の1枚を半分に折る。うらも同じに。

Fold up the top flap, turn over and repeat.

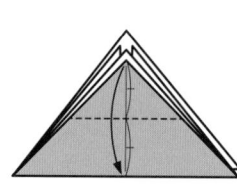

4

上の1枚を谷折りする。残りの3か所も同じに。

Fold down the top flap. Repeat on the remaining three faces.

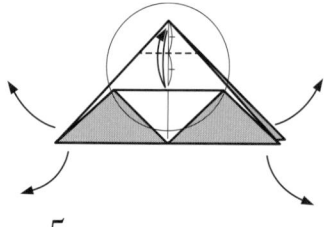

5

上の三角の半分のところで折りすじをつける。4つのかどを持って開く。

Fold the top triangle in half to make a crease. Pull open the four corners.

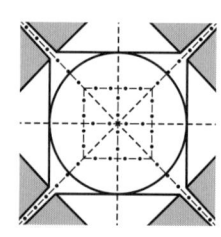

6

中心の折りすじを図のようにつけ直す。中心を沈めるように折る。

Refold the center creases as shown, then fold the center in.

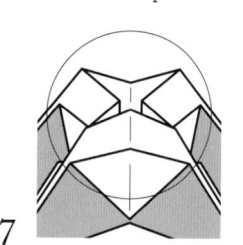

7

折りすじどおりに折ったところ。

Fold along the creases.

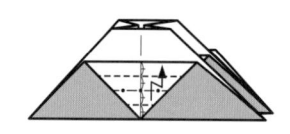

8

上の1枚に折りすじをつけ、段折り（P. 16）する。残りの3か所も同じに。

Make creases on the top flap to do a pleat fold (page 16). Repeat on the other three flaps.

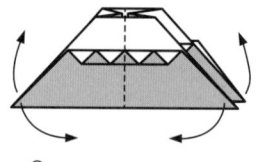

9

まん中の折りすじを谷折りして、立体にする。

Fold along the dotted line so it stands up.

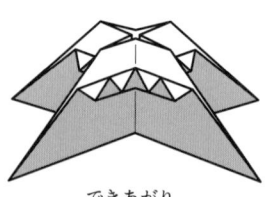

できあがり
Finished!

相撲取り Sumo Wrestler [see page 25]

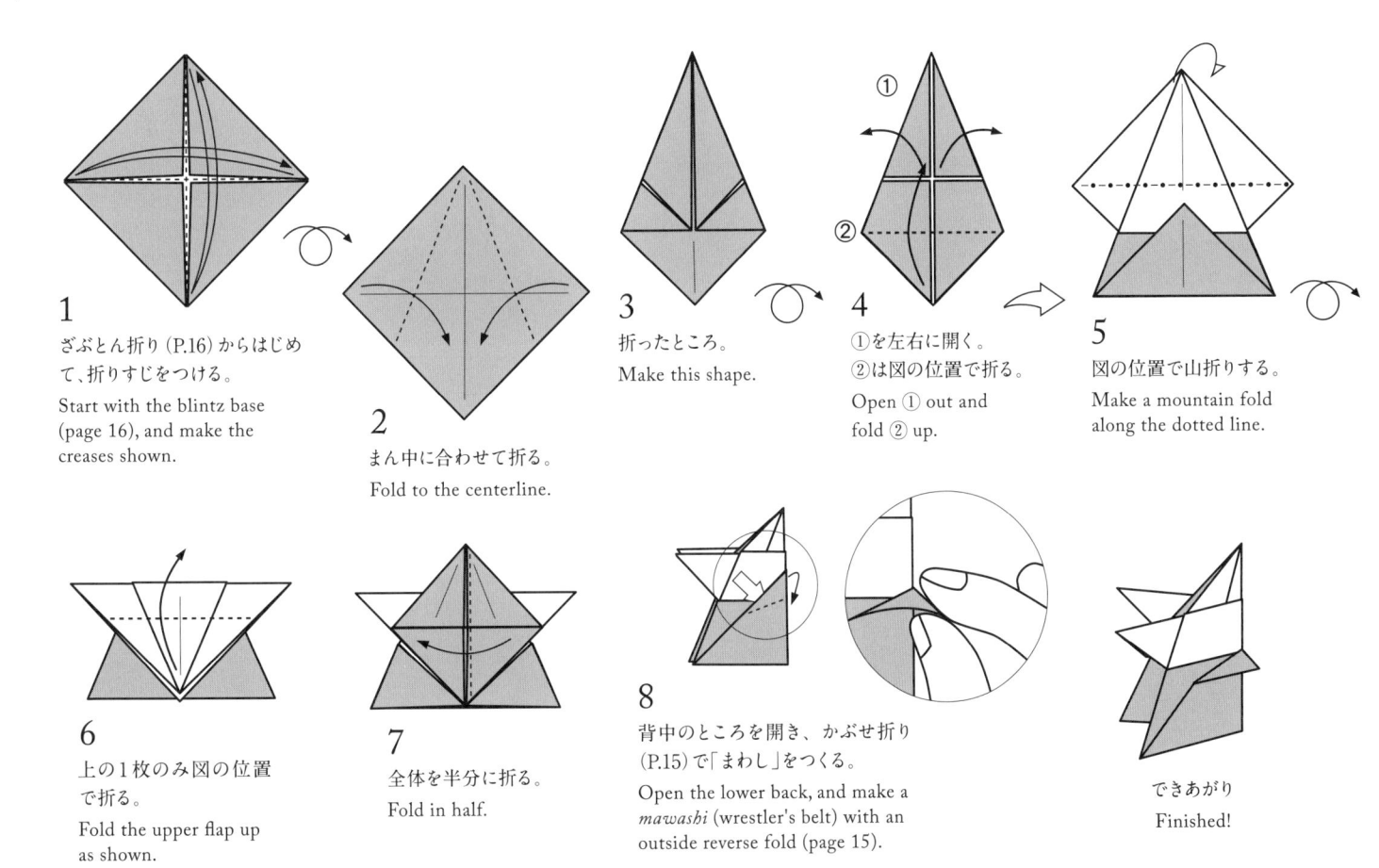

1

ざぶとん折り（P.16）からはじめ
て、折りすじをつける。

Start with the blintz base
(page 16), and make the
creases shown.

2

まん中に合わせて折る。

Fold to the centerline.

3

折ったところ。

Make this shape.

4

①を左右に開く。
②は図の位置で折る。

Open ① out and
fold ② up.

5

図の位置で山折りする。

Make a mountain fold
along the dotted line.

6

上の1枚のみ図の位置
で折る。

Fold the upper flap up
as shown.

7

全体を半分に折る。

Fold in half.

8

背中のところを開き、かぶせ折り
（P.15）で「まわし」をつくる。

Open the lower back, and make a
mawashi (wrestler's belt) with an
outside reverse fold (page 15).

できあがり
Finished!

鬼 Oni [see page 27] ✂

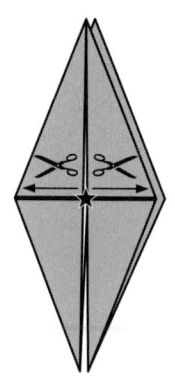

1

鶴（P.65-66）の8の形まで折る。左右が分かれているほうを下にする。上の1枚だけつまんで、★のところから左右のかどまで切り込みを入れる。うらも同じに。

Start from the Crane step 8 (page 65-66). Place the end with the split down. Cut a slit from the ★ to each corner, on the top flap only. Repeat on the back.

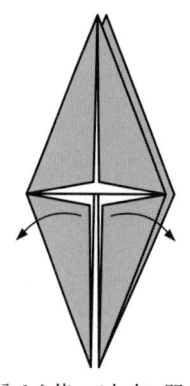

2

切り込みを使って左右に開く。うらも同じに。

Open both sides under the slits. Repeat on the back.

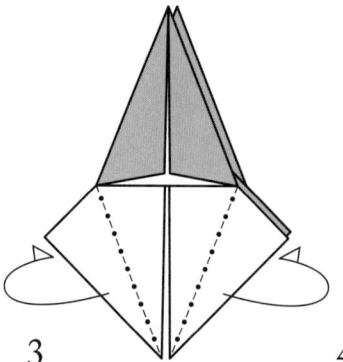

3

開いた部分を山折りで内側に折り込む。うらも同じにする。

Fold the flaps back and in. Repeat on the back.

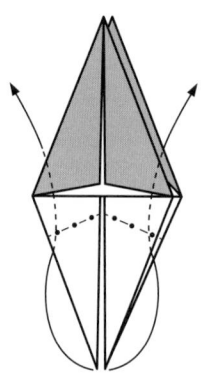

4

左右で中わり折り（P.15）をしてツノをつくる。

Make an inside reverse fold (page 15) on both sides to create horns.

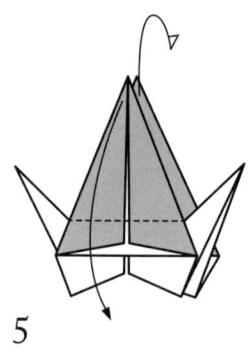

5

上の1枚を図の位置で折る。うらはそのまま折り下げる。

Fold the top flap along the dotted line. Fold the back flap all the way down.

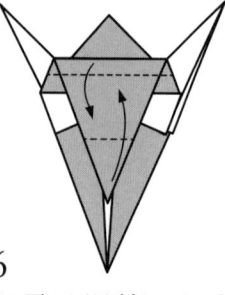

6

先に下のかどを折り、その上にかぶせて上の辺を折る。

Fold the bottom corner up, then fold the top flap down over it.

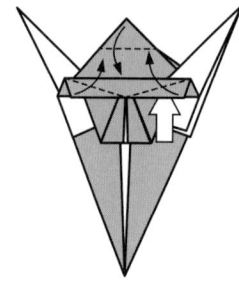

7

上のかどを図の位置で折る。⇨のところで開いて左右のはしを折り上げる。

Fold the top corner along the dotted line. Open at the ⇨ and fold up the left and right sides.

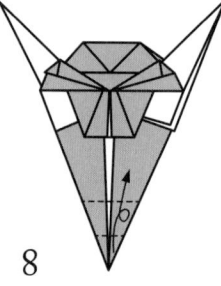

8

下のかどを2回折る。

Fold the bottom corner up twice.

できあがり
Finished!

豆入れ Bean Holder [see page 29]

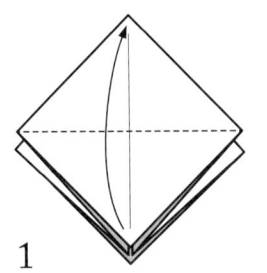

1

四角折り（P.15）からはじめて、上の1枚を半分に折る。うらも同じに。

Start with the square base (page 15), with the patterned side in. Fold the top flap in half and repeat on the back.

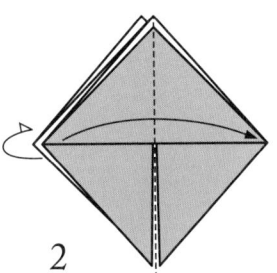

2

上の1枚を右に折る。うらも同じに。

Fold one side to the right. Turn over and repeat.

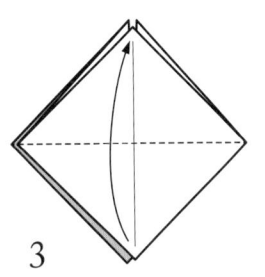

3

上の1枚を半分に折る。うらも同じに。

Fold up the top flap, turn over and repeat.

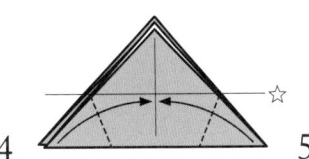

4

☆印の線に合わせるように、左右のはしを折る。うらも同じに。

Fold the left and right sides so they meet the ☆line shown. Turn over and repeat.

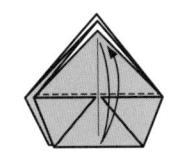

5

上の1枚に折りすじをつける。うらも同じに。4の形に戻す。

Create a valley crease on the top flap. Turn over and repeat. Unfold to the shape of step 4.

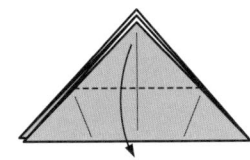

6

5でつけた折り線を使って折る。うらも同じに。

Fold using the crease created in step 5. Turn over and repeat.

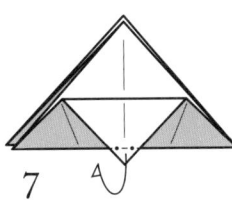

7

かどを山折りする。うらも同じに。

Mountain fold the tip. Turn over and repeat.

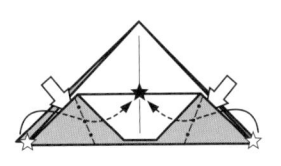

8

4でつけた折り線を山折りして、☆が★につくように中わり折り（P.15）する。うらも同じに。

Inside reverse fold (page 15) so the ☆s meet the ★ by mountain folding along the creases made in step 4. Repeat on the back.

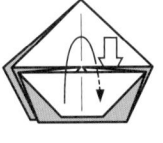

9

上の1枚を矢印の中に差しこむ。うらも同じに。あいだの2か所も5、6、7、9と同じに折る。

Slip the top part in where the arrow shows. Turn over and repeat. Fold the two remaining flaps as in 5, 6, 7 and 9.

10

折りすじをつけてから、底を押して、中を開いて形をととのえる。

After making a crease, squash the bottom down while opening to make a box shape.

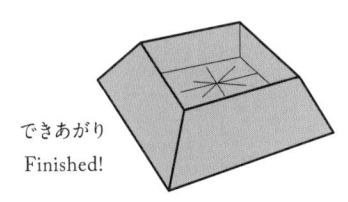

できあがり
Finished!

女雛 Mebina [see page 31]

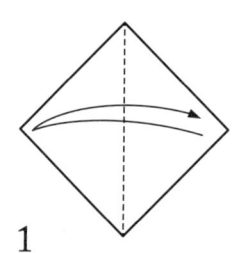

1

うら（白）を上にして、折り
すじをつける。

Place the white side up,
and make a crease as
shown.

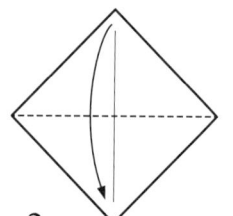

2

半分に折る。

Fold in half .

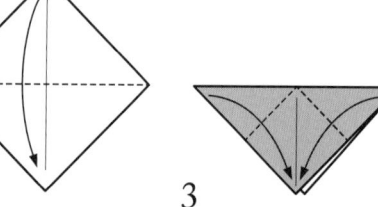

3

まん中の折りすじに合わ
せて左右のかどを折る。

Fold each side in to the
center crease.

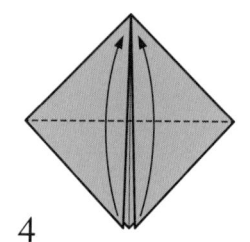

4

左右の上の紙だけを折る。

Fold the top flap up on
both sides.

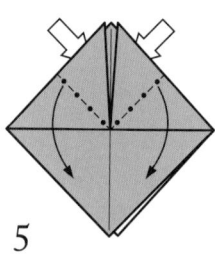

5

⇨のところで開いて、
下に広げてたたむ。

Open at the ⇨ and
⇨, then squash down.

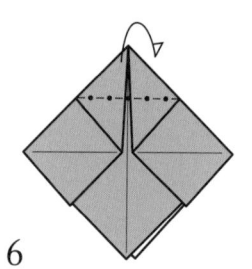

6

上のかどを山折りする。

Mountain fold the top
corner back.

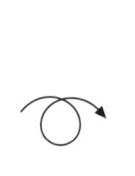

7

三角形の部分を上から
3分の1のところで折る。

Fold the triangle up at
1/3 from the top.

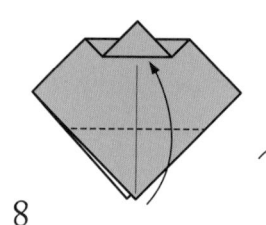

8

7で折った線に合わせ、下の
かどを2枚いっしょに折る。

Fold both bottom flaps up
to the edge made in step 7.

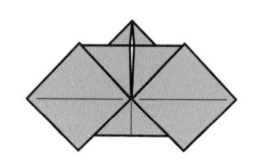

できあがり

Finished!

男雛 Obina [see page 33]

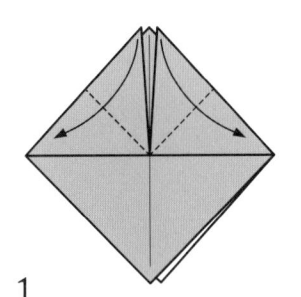

1

めびなの4を折ったところからはじめる。左右の上の紙を三角に折る。

Start from the Mebina step 4. Fold the top flaps on both sides down into small triangles.

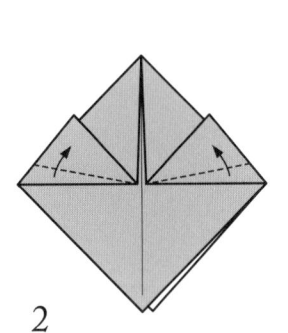

2

図の位置ではしを少し折る。

Fold the edges up a little as shown.

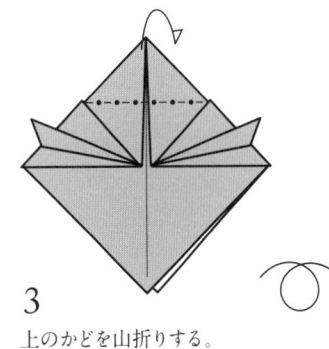

3

上のかどを山折りする。

Fold the upper corner back.

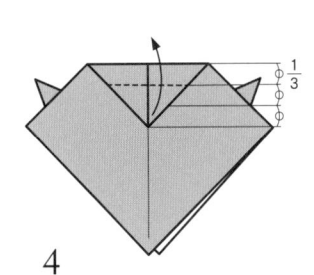

4

三角の部分を上から3分の1のところで折る。

Fold the triangle up at 1/3 from the top.

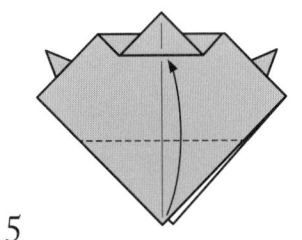

5

4で折った線に合わせ、下のかどを2枚いっしょに折る。

Fold both bottom flaps up to the edge made in step 4.

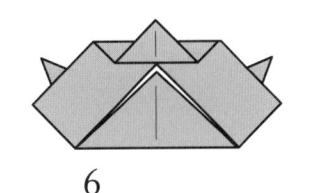

6

折ったところ。

Make this shape.

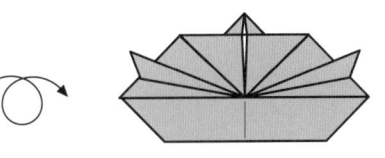

できあがり
Finished!

桜 Sakura [see page 35] ✂

＊紙は4分の1の大きさにカットして使います（うらに指示線あり）。桜の花が4つできます。

Cut the paper into quarters before starting (there are guide lines on the back). You can make 4 flowers.

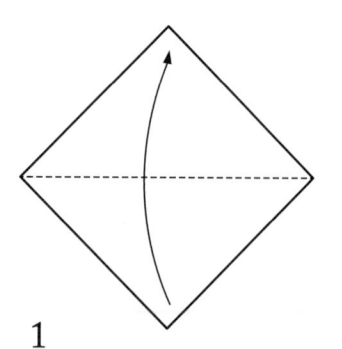

1

うら（白）を上にして半分に折る。

Place the white back side up
and fold in half.

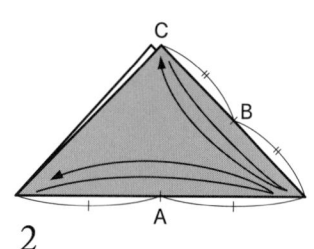

2

2辺それぞれを図のようにかるく
折って、半分の位置（A、B）に印
をつける。

Fold gently to each corner as
shown and make marks at the
half way points A and B.

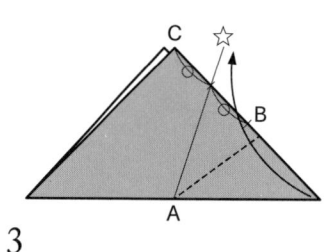

3

BとCのまん中に印をつける。Aと☆
の線に合うように、かどを谷折りする。

Make a mark half way between
B and C. Valley fold the corner
so its edge meets the line from A to ☆.

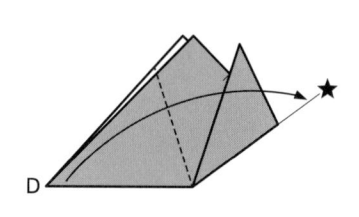

4

Dが★の線に合うように谷折りする。

Valley fold so D meets the ★ mark.

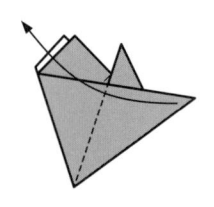

5

上の1枚を図の位置で折る。

Fold the top flap along the
dotted line.

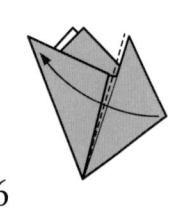

6

図の位置で谷折りする。

Valley fold along the
dotted line.

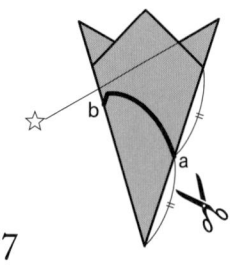

7

☆の線を目安に、太線をaからb
までハサミで切る。

Cut along the line shown from a
to b, using the ☆ line as a marker.

8

切って、開いたところ。

After cutting and opening.

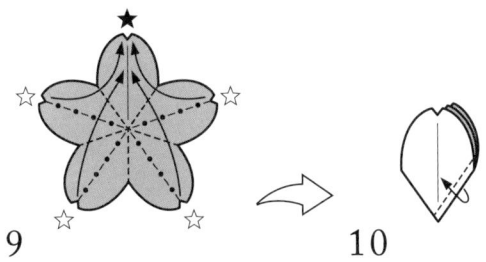

9

折りすじを図のように変えて、
☆が★につくようにたたむ。

Change the creases as
shown, then fold so the ☆s
meet the ★.

10

はしを5ミリ程度まと
めて折る。

Fold all the edges up
at once, about 5mm.

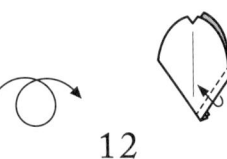

11

折ったところ。

Make this shape.

12

10と同様にはしを折る。

Repeat step 10.

13

上の1枚を下に開きなが
ら、全体を開く。

Pull the top flap down
to open the flower.

14

開いたところ。

Make this shape.

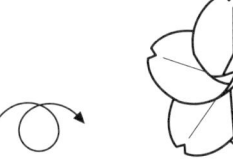

15

中心を五角形になるようにつぶす。

Squash the center into a
pentagon shape.

16

つぶしたところ。

After squashing.

できあがり

Finished!

侍 Samurai [see page 37]

アレンジ／渡部浩美
Arranged by Hiromi Watabe

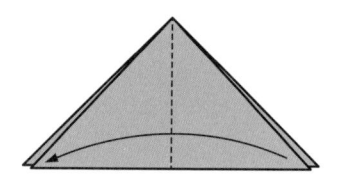

1

三角折り（P.15）からはじめる。
1枚を左に折る。

Start with the triangle base (page 15), and fold one flap to the left.

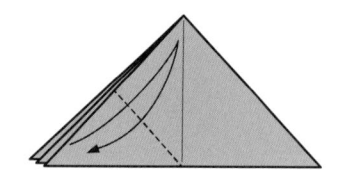

2

折りすじをつける。

Make a crease.

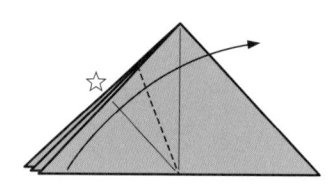

3

2で折った折りすじ☆をまん中の線に合うように折る。

Fold so the ☆ crease made in step 2 meets the center line.

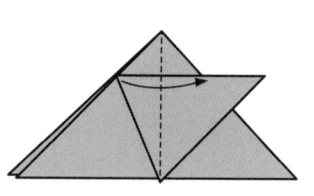

4

折ったところ。さらに1枚を右へ折る。

Make this shape, and fold the flap to the right.

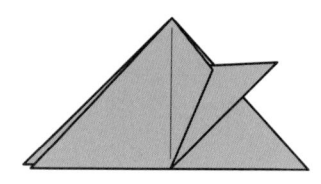

5

左側も1〜4と同様に折る。

Repeat steps 1 to 4 on the left.

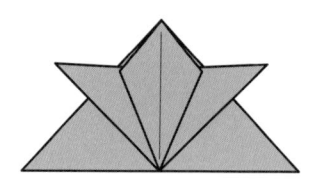

6

折ったところ。

Make this shape.

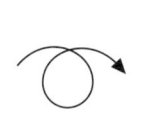

7

上の1枚を左へ折る。

Fold the top flap to the left.

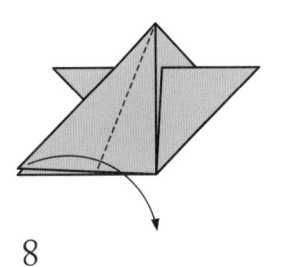

8

上の1枚をまん中に合わせ
て折る。

Fold the top flap to the
center.

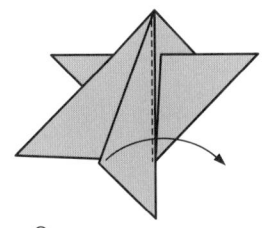

9

さらに折る。

Fold again.

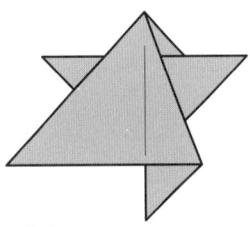

10

左側も7〜9と同様に折る
（左右は反対に）。

Repeat steps 7 to 9 on
the left, reversing the left
and right.

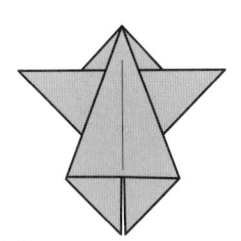

11

折ったところ。

Make this shape.

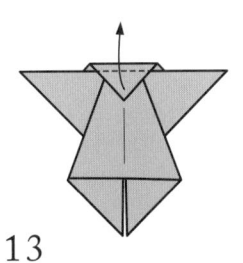

12

図の位置で折る。

Fold along the dotted line.

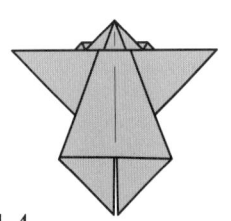

13

図の位置で折る。

Fold along the dotted line.

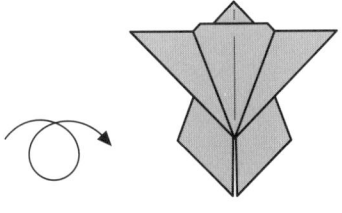

14

折ったところ。

Make this shape.

できあがり
Finished!

兜 Kabuto [see page 39]

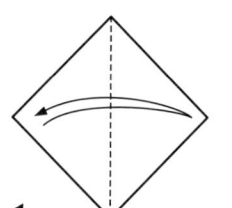

1
半分に折って折り
すじをつける。

Fold in half to
crease.

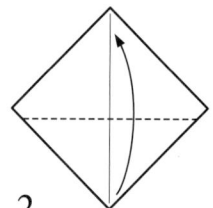

2
上を少しあけて谷折
りする。

Leaving a little
extra room in the
top half,
make a valley fold.

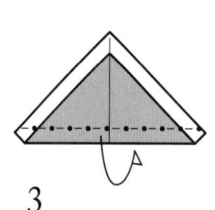

3
下を山折りする。

Make a mountain
fold on the bottom.

4
☆と★がつくように谷
折りする。

Make a valley fold so
the ☆s meet the ★.

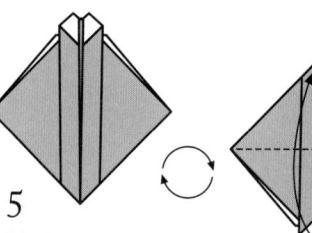

5
折ったところ。

Make this shape.

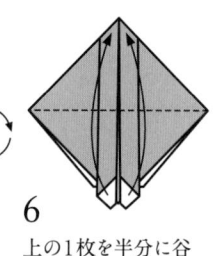

6
上の1枚を半分に谷
折りする。

Fold the top layer in
half in a valley fold.

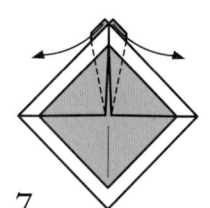

7
図のように斜めに谷
折りする。

Make a diagonal
valley fold as shown
in the diagram.

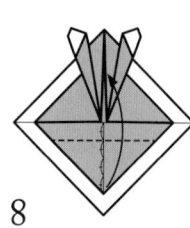

8
上の1枚を4分の1の
ところで谷折りする。

Make a valley fold
on the top flap at
the 1/4 point.

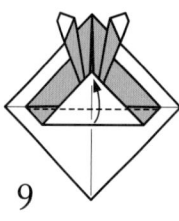

9
図のように上の2
枚を折り上げる。

Fold the top two
layers upward as
shown.

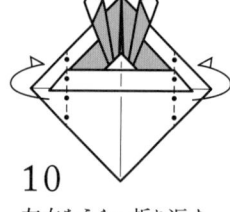

10
左右をうらへ折り返す。

Fold the left and
right sides to the back.

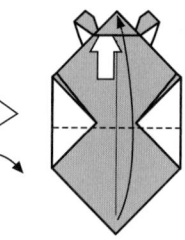

11
半分に折り、あい
だを開いて三角の
中へ差しこむ。

Fold in half and
tuck the corner
inside the triangle.

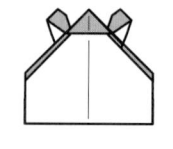

12
差しこんだところ。

View with the
corner tucked in.

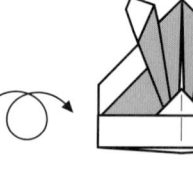

できあがり
Finished!

鯉 Koi [see page 41]

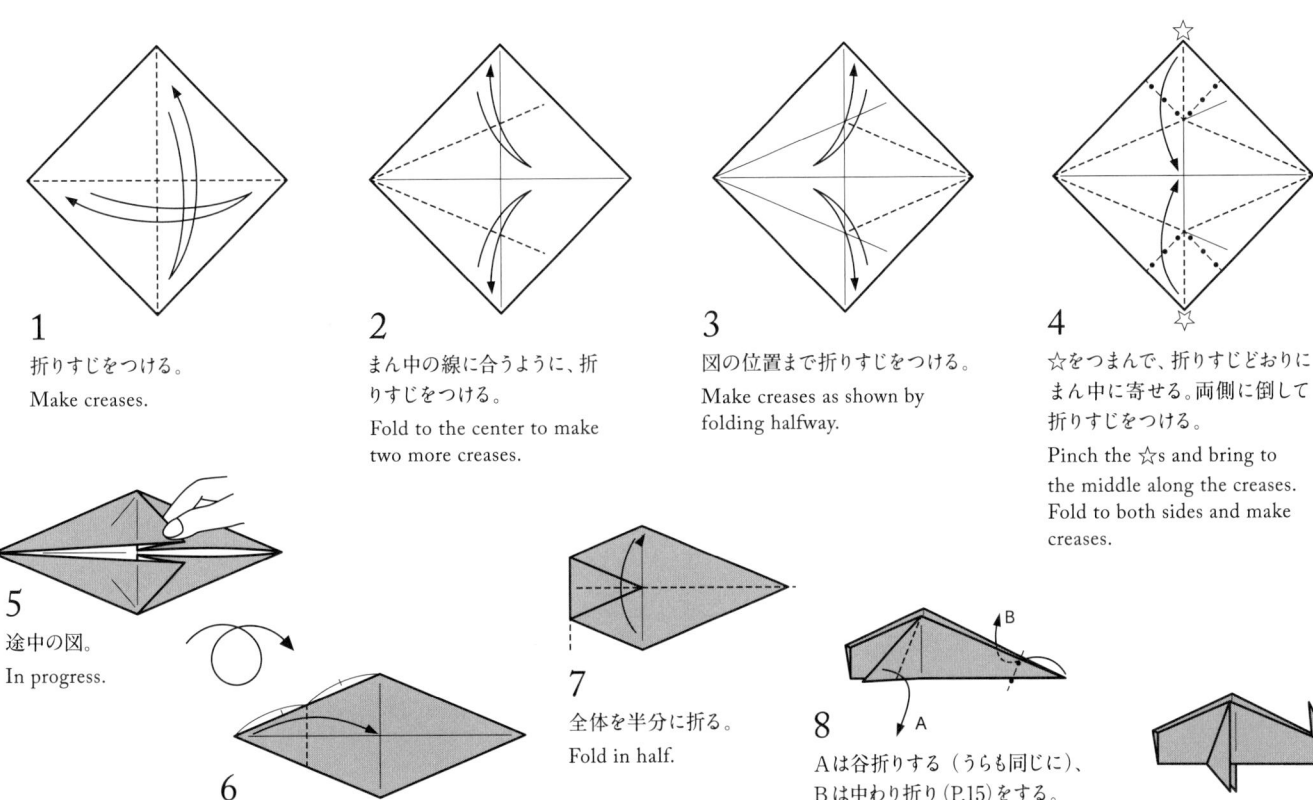

1

折りすじをつける。

Make creases.

2

まん中の線に合うように、折りすじをつける。

Fold to the center to make two more creases.

3

図の位置まで折りすじをつける。

Make creases as shown by folding halfway.

4

☆をつまんで、折りすじどおりにまん中に寄せる。両側に倒して折りすじをつける。

Pinch the ☆s and bring to the middle along the creases. Fold to both sides and make creases.

5

途中の図。

In progress.

6

図の位置で折る。

Fold as shown.

7

全体を半分に折る。

Fold in half.

8

Aは谷折りする（うらも同じに）、Bは中わり折り（P.15）をする。

Create a valley fold at A, and an inside reverse fold (page 15) at B. Repeat A on the back.

できあがり

Finished!

蝸牛 Snail [see page 43]

かたつむり

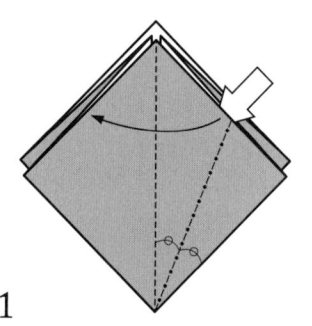

1

四角折り(P.15)からはじめる。4つある
ひだに折りすじをつけて、指を入れて
開いて、つぶす。

Start with the square base (page 15).
Add creases to all four flaps as
shown, then insert a finger and
squash open.

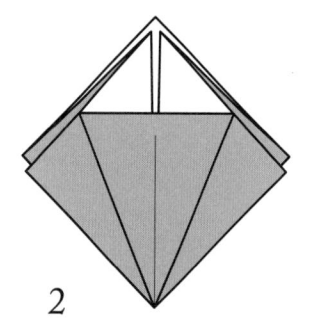

2

1つ折ったところ。残りの
3か所のひだも同じに。

Fold the remaining 3
flaps in the same way.

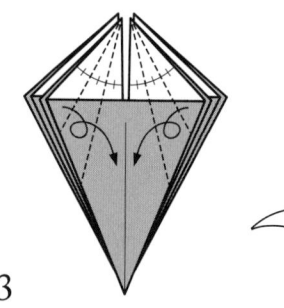

3

かどを3等分して谷折りを2回
する。うらも同じに。

Create two valley folds so the
corners are folded in thirds.
Do the same on the back side.

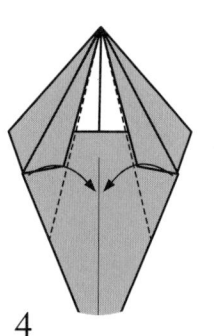

4

途中の図。
In progress.

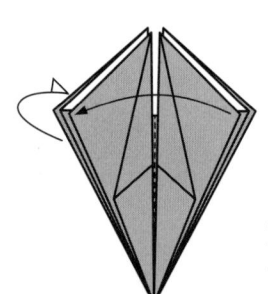

5

2枚左へおくって、うらが見
えているかどが出てきたら、
3と同じに谷折りを2回す
る。うらも同じに。

Fold two flaps to the left.
A corner with the back
visible will appear. Fold in
thirds as in step 3. Turn
over and repeat.

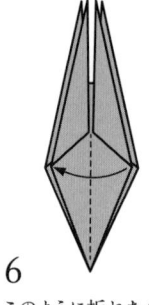

6

このように折れたら、
1枚左へおくる。

After folding like
this, fold one flap to
the left.

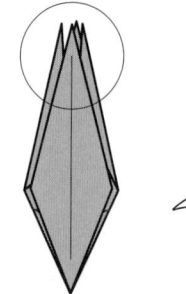

7

とがった先が4つあることを
確認して、中の2つを中わり
折り(p.15)する。

Fold 2 of 4 points using an
inside reverse fold (page 15).

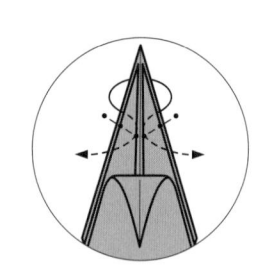

とがった先を、左と右に中
わり折りする。

Fold the points to the left
and right using an inside
reverse fold.

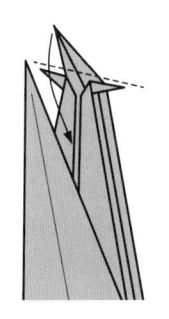

8

後ろのとがった先を手前
に折って、のりでとめる。

Fold the back point
forward and glue down.

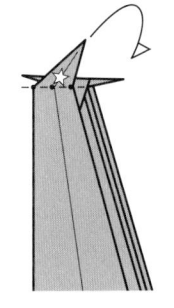

9

☆の部分を折って、8で
折ったところにかぶせて、
のりでとめる。

Fold the part marked
by a ☆ over the top as
shown and glue down.

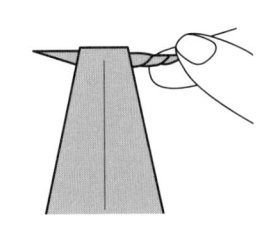

10

ツノの先をねじる。

Twist the feelers.

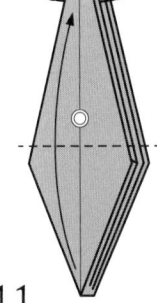

ここで折る
（かどの少し上）
Fold here
(slightly above the corner).

11

図の位置で谷折りして、◎のとこ
ろにのり貼る。

Valley fold along the dotted line,
then attach with glue at the ◎.

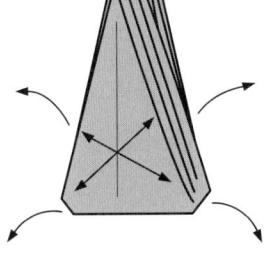

12

矢印同士で引っぱりながら、
ふくらませる。

Pull in the direction of the
arrows and inflate.

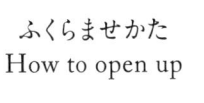

ふくらませかた
How to open up

a

左の手で、首に近い紙を持つ。

Pinch the layer nearest the
neck with your left hand.

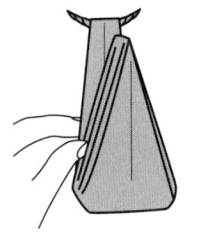

b

右の手はいちばん外側を持ち、
斜めに少しずつ引っぱって、
全体をふくらませる。

Next use your right hand to
pinch the outermost layer
and pull out bit by bit to
open up.

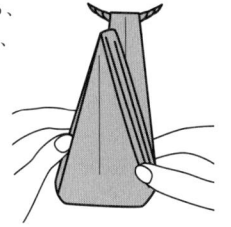

c

残ったところを引っぱり、形をととのえる。

Pull out the remaining layers to make a ball.

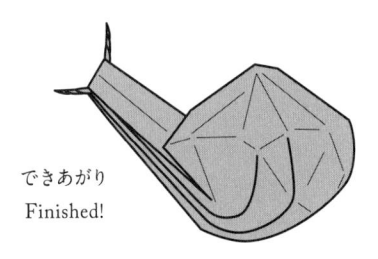

できあがり
Finished!

蝶 Butterfly [see page 45]

ちょう

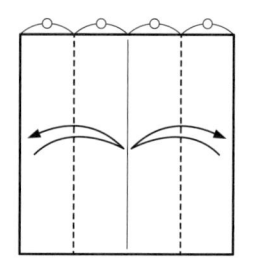

1

半分に折り、折りすじをつけ
てから、残りの折りすじをつ
ける。

Fold in half to make the
center crease, then fold
each side in half to make 2
more creases.

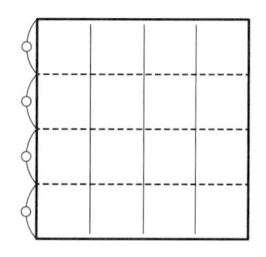

2

1と同様に、横にも4等分
の折りすじをつける。

Fold horizontally in
the same way as step 1
to divide into quarters.

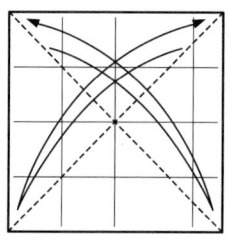

3

対角線に折りすじをつける。

Add creases on the
diagonals.

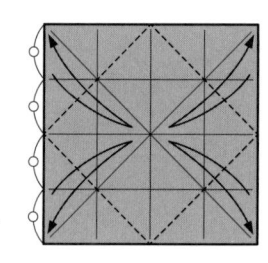

4

かどが中心に合うように折っ
て、折りすじをつける。

Fold the corners into
the center to make creases.

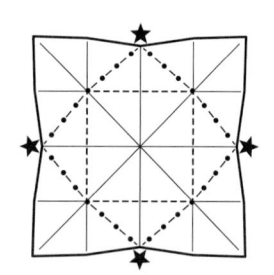

5

1〜4までにつけた折りすじ
を使って、★が中心に集まる
ように折りたたむ。

Using the creases created
in steps 1 to 4, fold so the
★s come into the center.

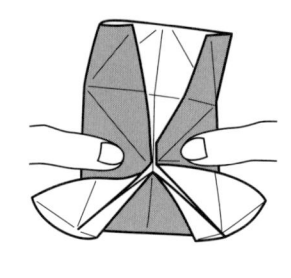

6

途中の図。

In progress.

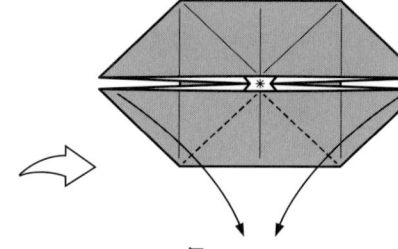

7

図の位置で折る。

Fold as shown.

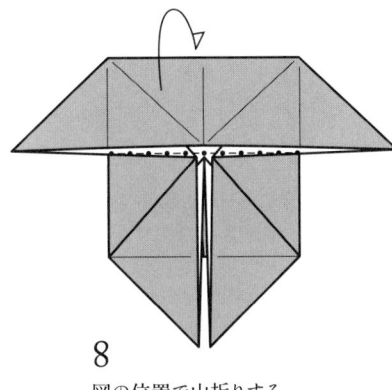

8

図の位置で山折りする。

Mountain fold as shown.

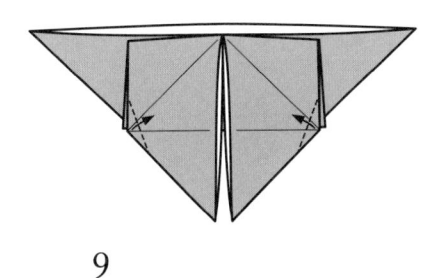

9

かどを少し折る。

Fold the corners a little.

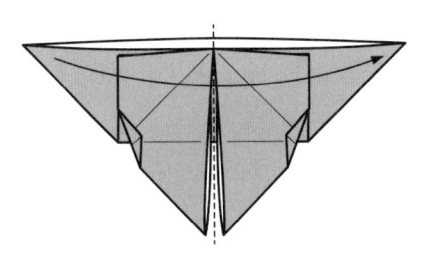

10

全体を半分に折る。

Fold in half.

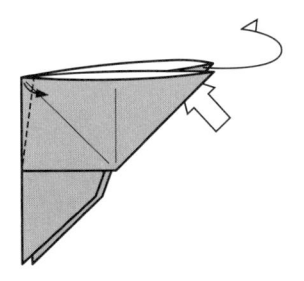

11

かどを斜めに谷折りしてから、後ろを開く。

Valley fold the left corner on the diagonal
and then open the back.

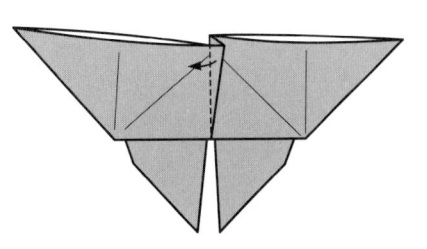

12

11で折った三角を左に折って立てる。

Fold the triangle made in
step 11 to the left and stand it up.

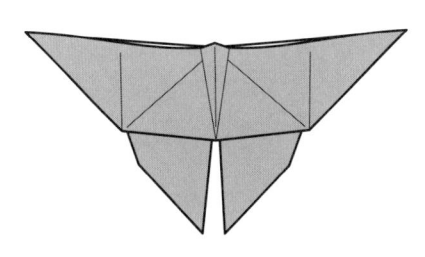

できあがり

Finished!

たとう Tato Pouch [see page 47]

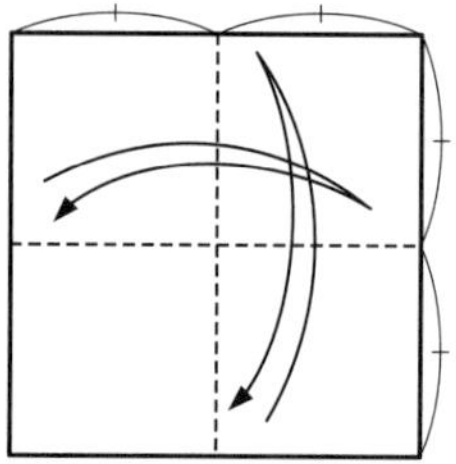

1

四角の折りすじをつける。

Create squares by making creases.

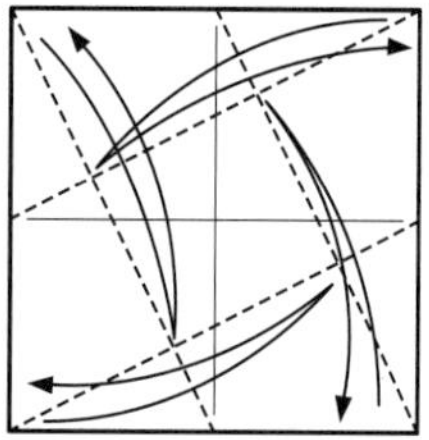

2

上下と左右に図の位置で斜めに折りすじをつける。

Make diagonal creases on the top and bottom, and left and right as shown.

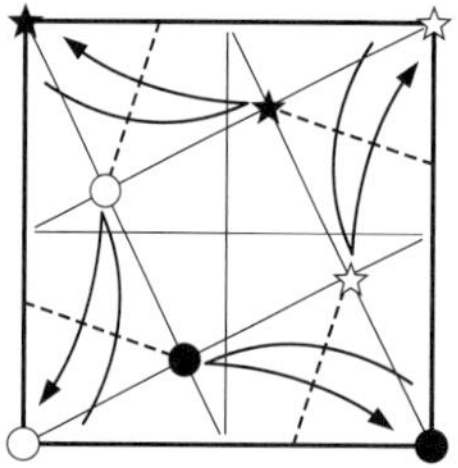

3

それぞれ、★と★、☆と☆、●と●、○と○が合うように折りすじをつける。

Make four more creases by bringing each of the two ★s, ☆s, ●s, and ○s together as shown.

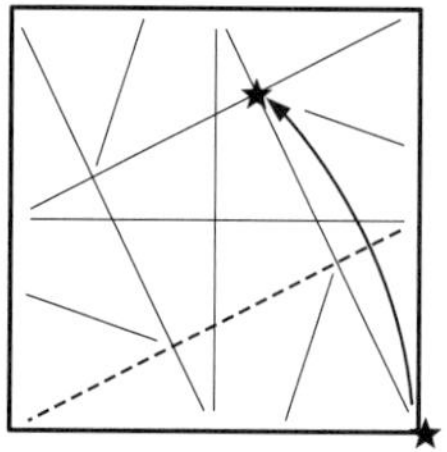

4

★と★が合うように折る。

Fold so the ★s match up.

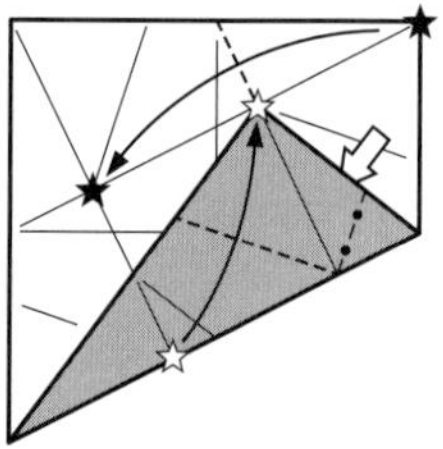

5

☆と☆、★と★がつくように、あいだを開いてたたむ。

Insert a finger at the arrow and open so the ☆s and ★s match up.

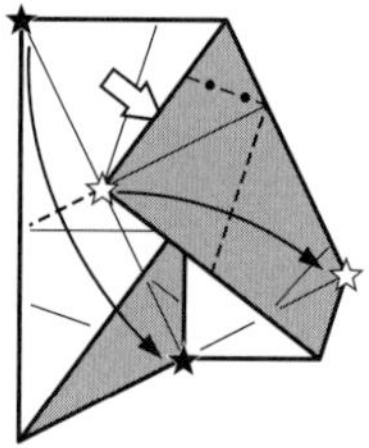

6

5と同様に、☆と☆、★と★がつくように、あいだを開いてたたむ。

Insert a finger at the arrow and fold so the ☆s and ★s match up, as in step 5.

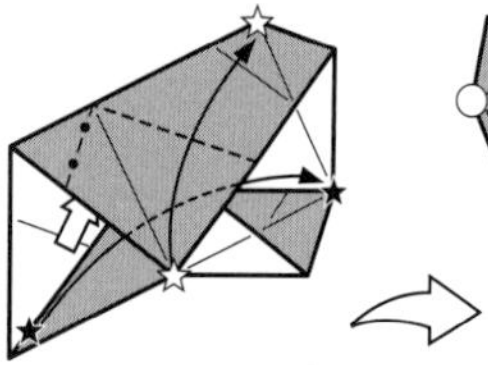

7

5・6と同様に☆と☆、★と★がつくように、あいだを開いてたたむ。

Insert a finger at the arrow and fold so the ☆s and ★s match up, as in step 5 and 6.

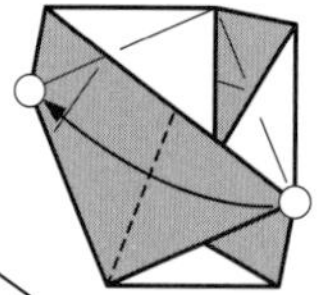

8

○が○につくように折る。

Fold so the ○s match up.

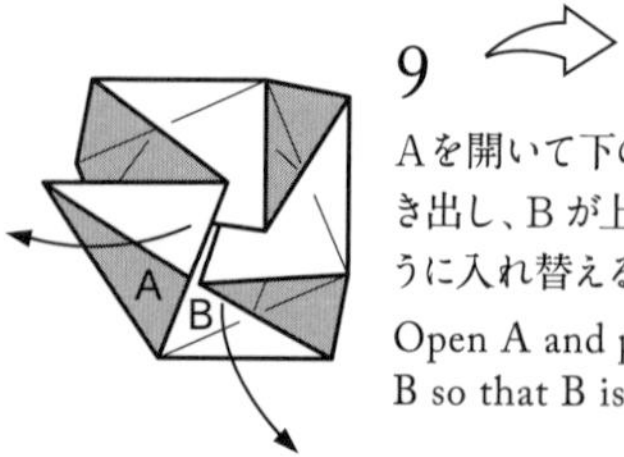

9

Aを開いて下のBを引き出し、Bが上になるように入れ替える。

Open A and pull out B so that B is on top.

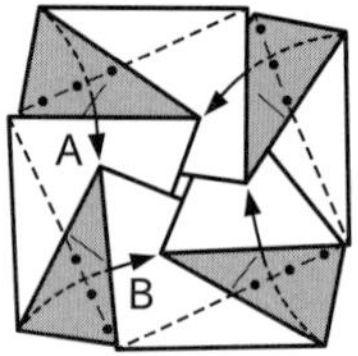

10

折りすじを使って、4か所ともかどを押し込む。

Using the creases, open and fold in each of the four corners.

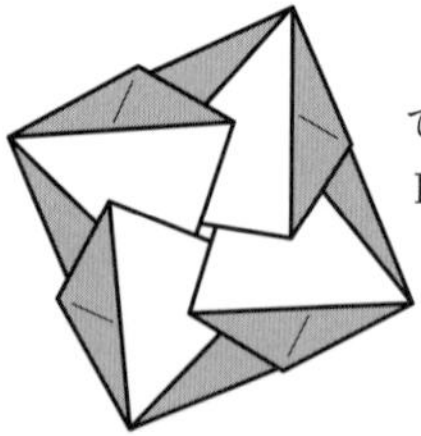

できあがり

Finished!

ぽち袋 Pochi Bag [see page 49]

アレンジ／渡部浩美
Arranged by Hiromi Watabe

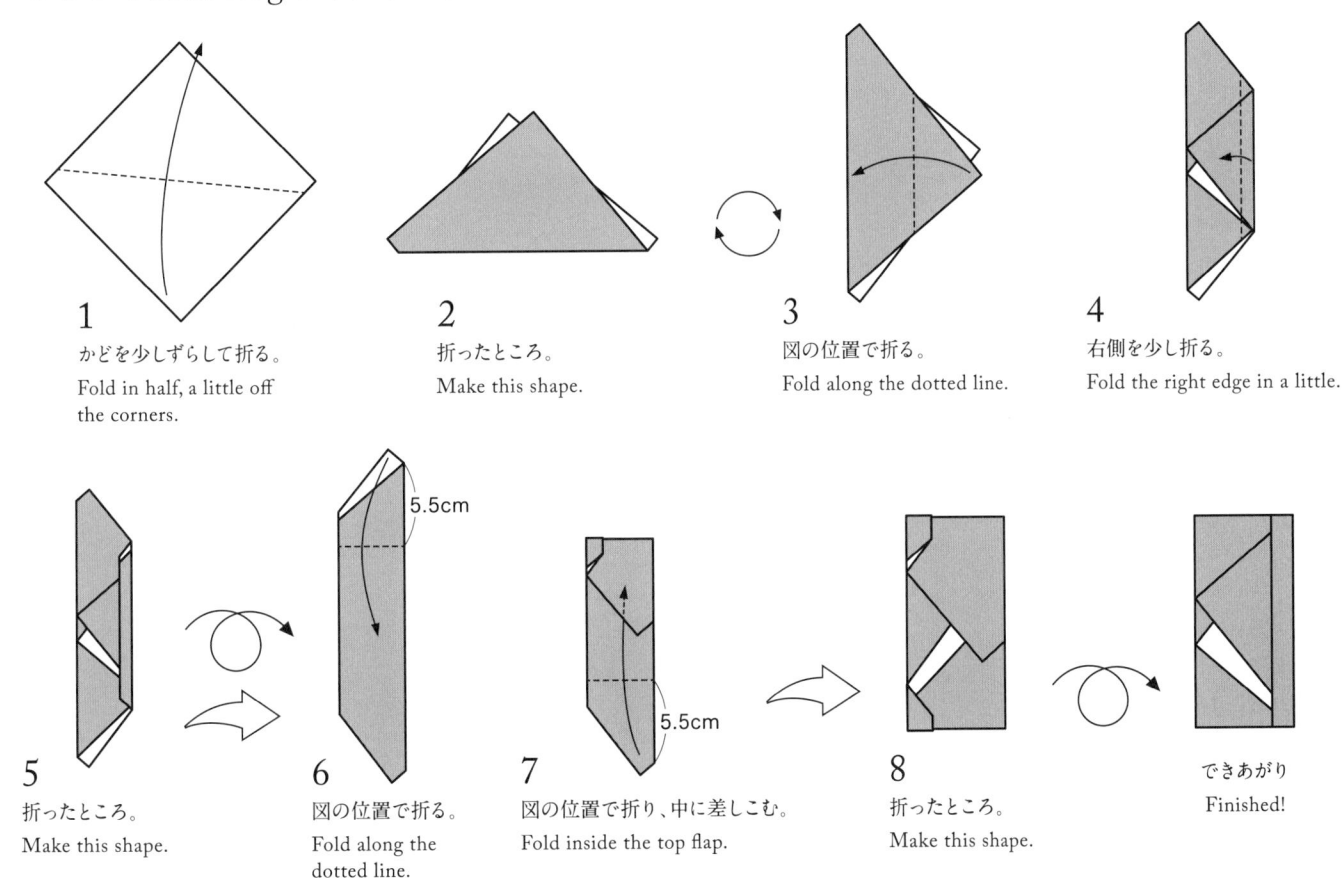

1
かどを少しずらして折る。
Fold in half, a little off the corners.

2
折ったところ。
Make this shape.

3
図の位置で折る。
Fold along the dotted line.

4
右側を少し折る。
Fold the right edge in a little.

5
折ったところ。
Make this shape.

6
図の位置で折る。
Fold along the dotted line.

7
図の位置で折り、中に差しこむ。
Fold inside the top flap.

8
折ったところ。
Make this shape.

できあがり
Finished!

箸袋 Chopstick Cover [see page 51]
<ruby>箸<rt>はし</rt>袋<rt>ぶくろ</rt></ruby>

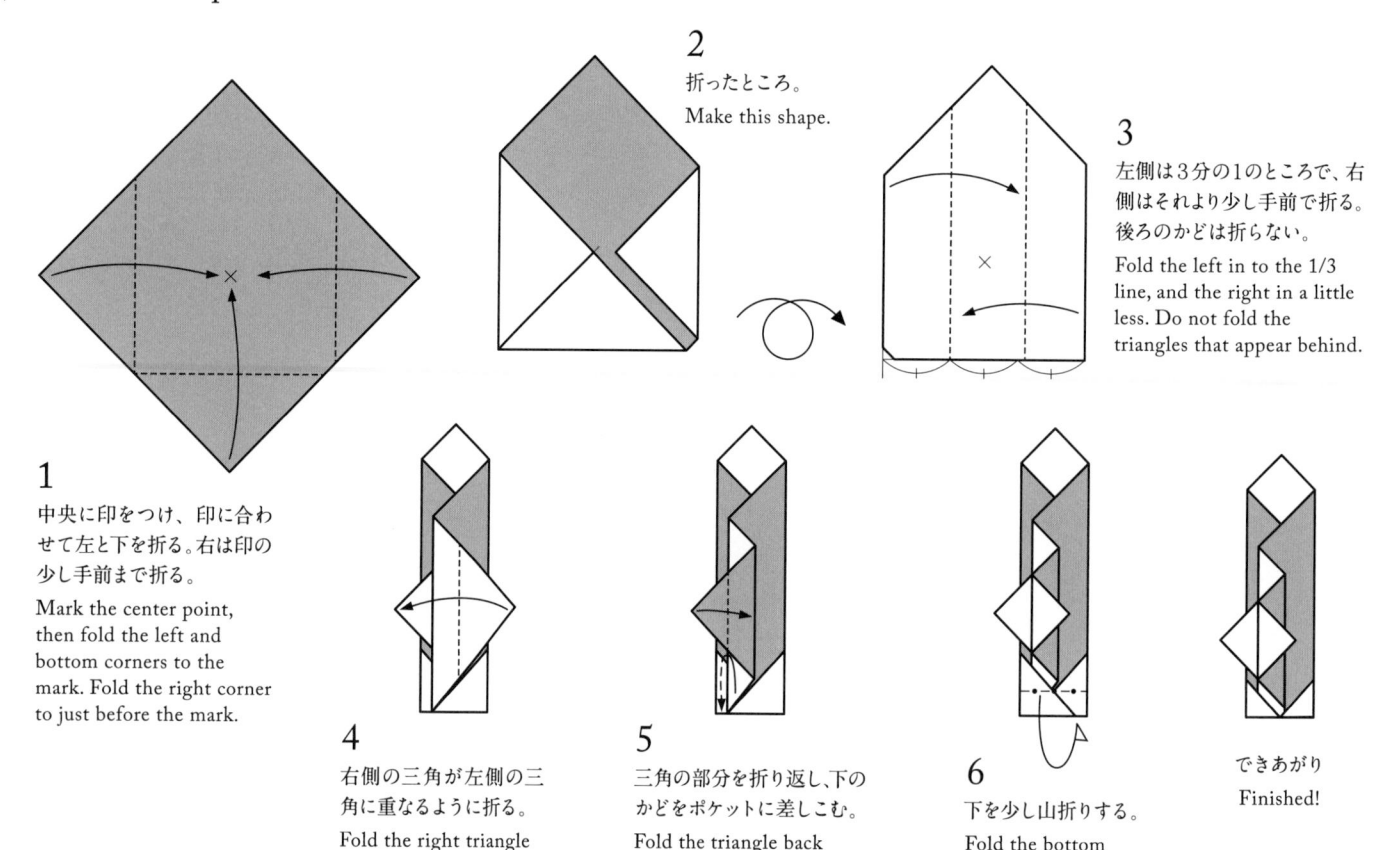

2

折ったところ。

Make this shape.

3

左側は3分の1のところで、右側はそれより少し手前で折る。後ろのかどは折らない。

Fold the left in to the 1/3 line, and the right in a little less. Do not fold the triangles that appear behind.

1

中央に印をつけ、印に合わせて左と下を折る。右は印の少し手前まで折る。

Mark the center point, then fold the left and bottom corners to the mark. Fold the right corner to just before the mark.

4

右側の三角が左側の三角に重なるように折る。

Fold the right triangle over the left triangle.

5

三角の部分を折り返し、下のかどをポケットに差しこむ。

Fold the triangle back again. Insert the bottom corner into the pouch.

6

下を少し山折りする。

Fold the bottom back as shown.

できあがり
Finished!

もみじ Momiji [see page 53]

[see page 53]

* 紙は4分の1の大きさにカットして使います（うらに指示線あり）。もみじが4つできます。
Cut the paper into quarters before starting (there are guide lines on the back). You can make 4 leaves.

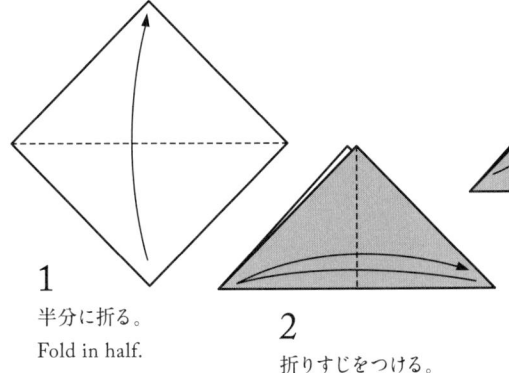

1
半分に折る。
Fold in half.

2
折りすじをつける。
Make a crease.

3
折りすじをつける。
Make creases.

4
3でつけた折りすじをつまんで、左からたたんでいく。このとき6のように少しずらしてたたむ。

Change the crease made in step 3 to a mountain fold, then fold in from the left, shifting a little as shown in step 6.

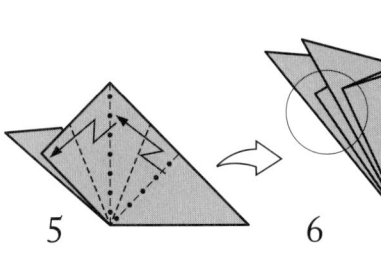

5
残りの2か所も2枚重ねたままたたんでいく。

Fold two more times, as shown.

6
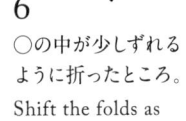
○の中が少しずれるように折ったところ。

Shift the folds as shown.

7
ハサミでこのように切り込みを入れる。上まで切らずに少しあける。

Use scissors to make a slit as shown. Don't cut all the way to the top.

切らない。
Don't cut.

8
切り込みのはしからハサミを入れ、このように切り落とす。はじめはまっすぐに切り（★のところ）、☆の線とぶつかるところから、ゆるくカーブさせて切る。必ず2つのかどの内側を切ること。切り落としたら、開いてまん中をへこませる。

Cut from the bottom of the slit as shown. First make a short straight cut up to the crease (the ★ part), and then cut in a loose curve after the ☆ line. Be sure to cut below the two corners. After cutting, open up and spread out.

できあがり
Finished!

鼠 ねずみ Mouse [see page 55] ✂

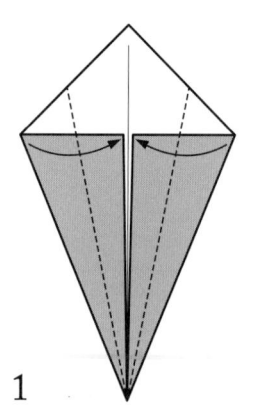

1

凪折り（P.16）からはじめる。
中央の線に合うように折る。

Start with the kite base (page 16).
Fold each side to the center.

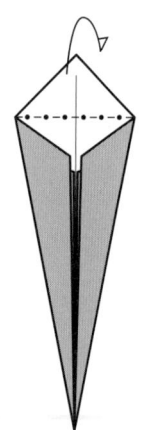

2

図のように山折りする。

Make a mountain fold
as shown.

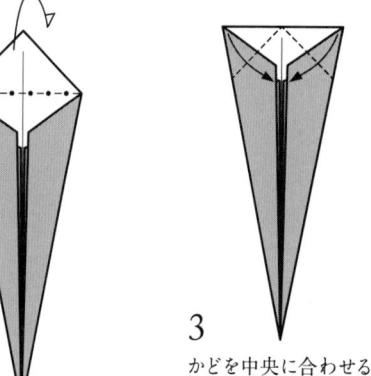

3

かどを中央に合わせる
ように折る。

Fold the corners over
to meet in the center.

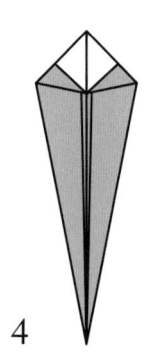

4

折ったところ。

Make this shape.

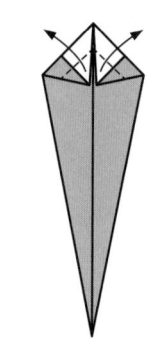

5

図の位置で折る。

Fold at the position shown.

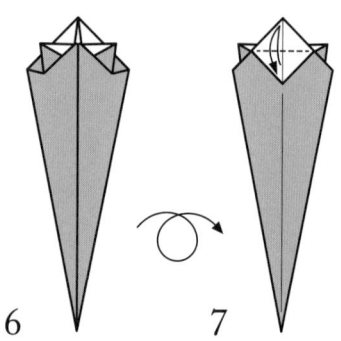

6

折ったところ。

Make this shape.

7

折りすじをつける。

Make a crease.

拡大図
Close-up

8

半分くらいまで切り込みを入
れてから、全体を半分に折る。

Cut a slit to the halfway
point, and then fold the
whole body in half.

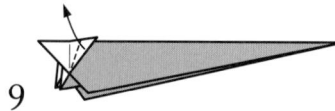

9

3で折った線に合わせて折る。
うらも同様に折る。

Fold along the crease created in step 3.
Do the same on the back.

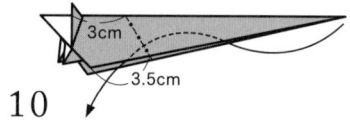

10

中わり折り（P.15）する。

Inside reverse fold (page 15).

3cm

3.5cm

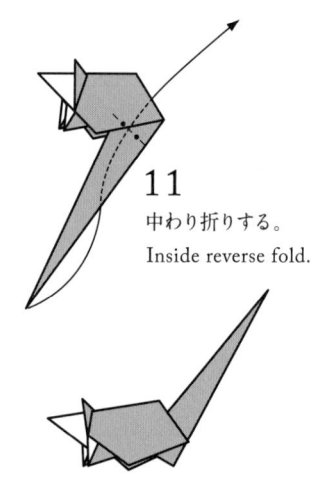

11

中わり折りする。

Inside reverse fold.

できあがり
Finished!

雉 Pheasant [see page 57]

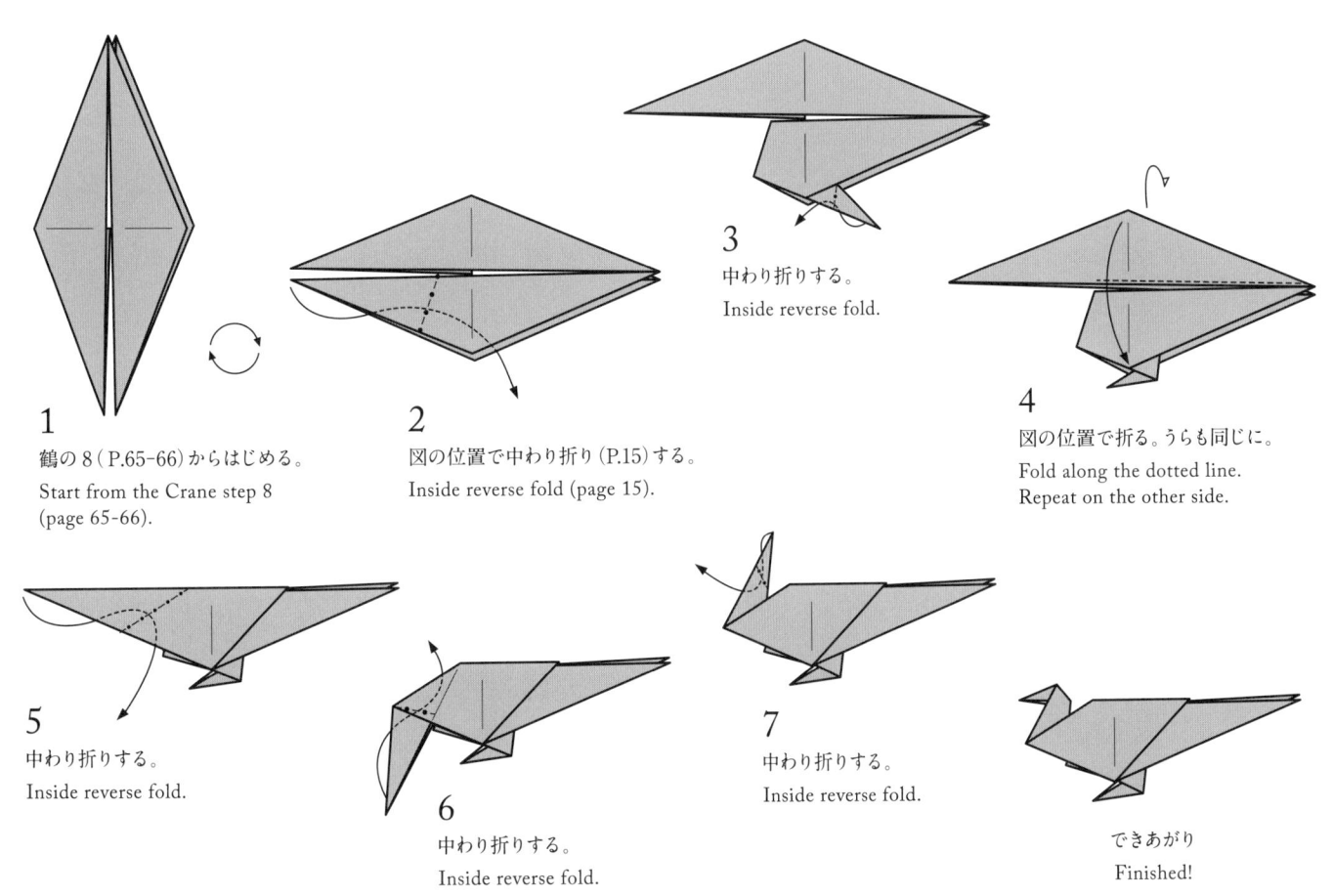

1
鶴の8（P.65-66）からはじめる。
Start from the Crane step 8
(page 65-66).

2
図の位置で中わり折り（P.15）する。
Inside reverse fold (page 15).

3
中わり折りする。
Inside reverse fold.

4
図の位置で折る。うらも同じに。
Fold along the dotted line.
Repeat on the other side.

5
中わり折りする。
Inside reverse fold.

6
中わり折りする。
Inside reverse fold.

7
中わり折りする。
Inside reverse fold.

できあがり
Finished!

亀 Turtle [see page 59]

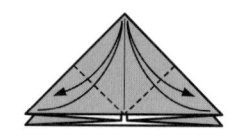

1

三角折り（P.15）からはじめる。左右のかどを中央の線に合わせて折り、折りすじをつける。

Start with the triangle base (page 15). Fold both corners to the center to make creases.

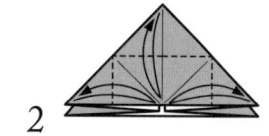

2

上の1枚だけ左右と上のかどを図のように折り、折りすじをつける。

Fold the left and right corners (top flap only) and the top corner to the center as shown to make creases.

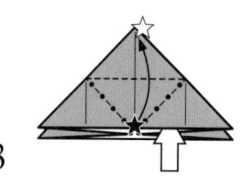

3

下のすき間を開き、下の辺★と上のかど☆を合わせるように折りたたむ。

Open from the bottom and fold so the ★ and meets the ☆ as shown.

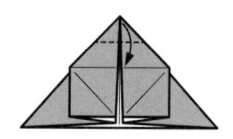

4

上の1枚だけ、下に折る。

Fold the top corner down (top flap only).

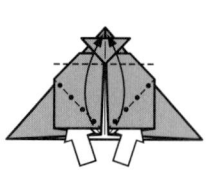

5

⇨の部分を開いて、図のように折りたたむ。

Open where the ⇨s are and squash.

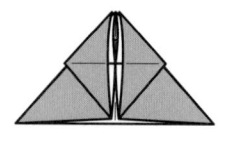

6

折ったところ。うらも1〜5と同じに折る。

Make this shape. Repeat steps 1 to 5 on the back.

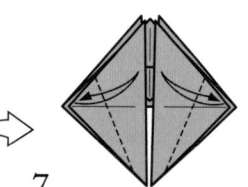

7

図のように折りすじをつける。

Fold as shown to make creases.

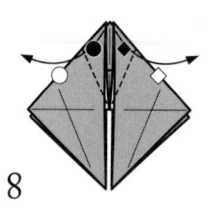

8

●と○、◆と◇がそれぞれ合うように折る。

Fold so the ● and ○ and the ◆ and ◇ meet.

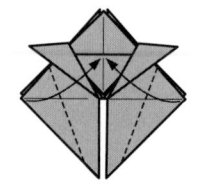

9

上の1枚だけ、左右のかどを7の折りすじにそって折る。うらも同じに折る。

Fold the left and right corners along the creases for the top layer only. Fold in the same way on the back.

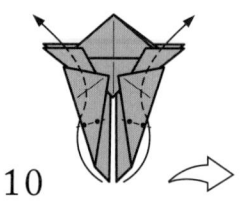

10

左右の下のかどを中わり折り（P.15）する。

Inside reverse fold (page 15) the lower points on the left and right.

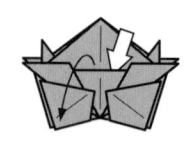

11

下から押しながら、⇨の部分を開く。左右をつまんで引き、形をととのえる。

While pushing from the bottom, open the ⇨ part. Next pull the left and right to adjust the shape.

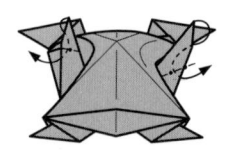

12

図の位置で中わり折りして、頭としっぽをつくる。

Inside reverse fold where shown to create the head and tail.

できあがり
Finished!

雪うさぎ Snow Rabbit [see page 61]

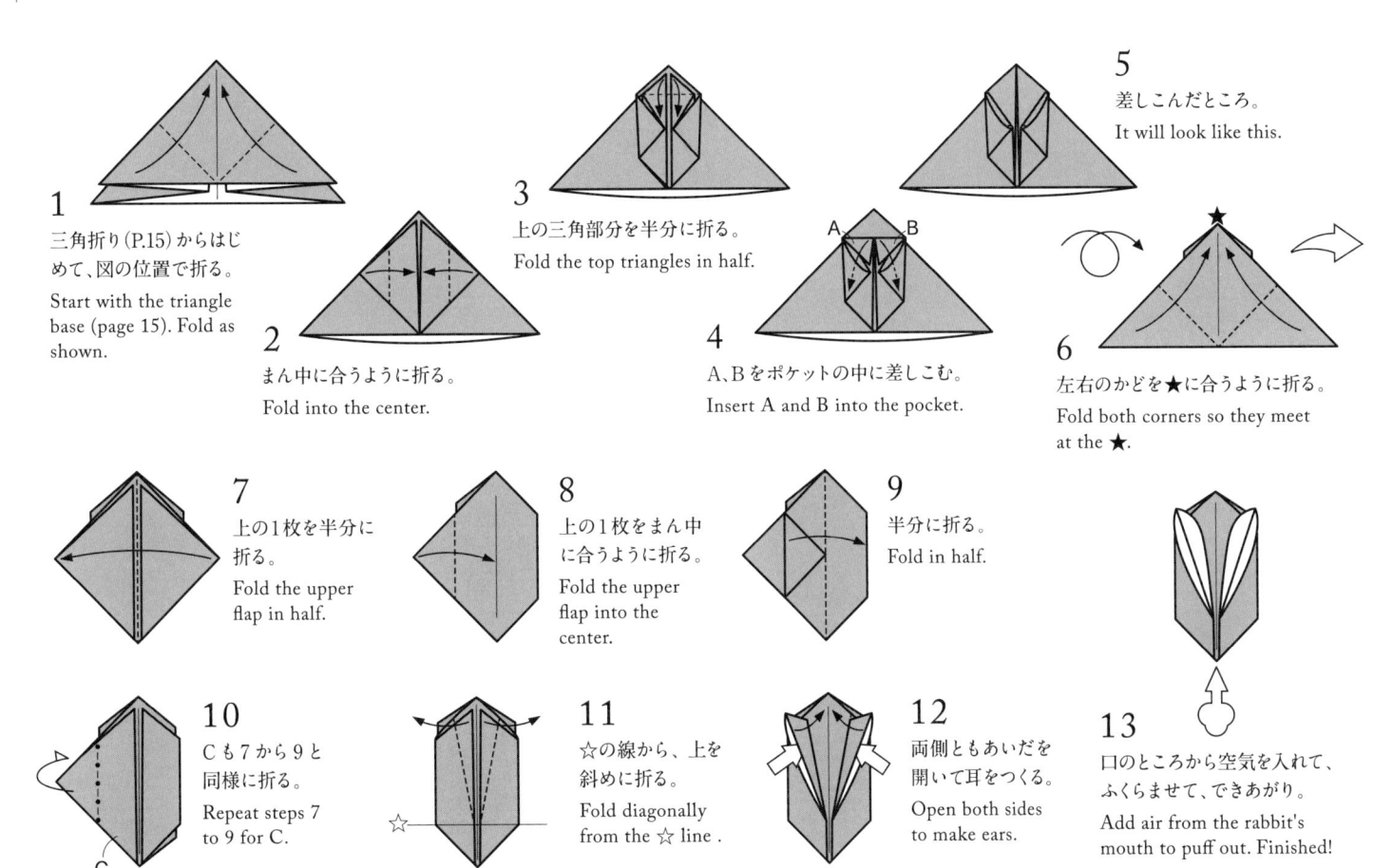

1

三角折り（P.15）からはじめて、図の位置で折る。

Start with the triangle base (page 15). Fold as shown.

2

まん中に合うように折る。

Fold into the center.

3

上の三角部分を半分に折る。

Fold the top triangles in half.

4

A、Bをポケットの中に差しこむ。

Insert A and B into the pocket.

5

差しこんだところ。

It will look like this.

6

左右のかどを★に合うように折る。

Fold both corners so they meet at the ★.

7

上の1枚を半分に折る。

Fold the upper flap in half.

8

上の1枚をまん中に合うように折る。

Fold the upper flap into the center.

9

半分に折る。

Fold in half.

10

Cも7から9と同様に折る。

Repeat steps 7 to 9 for C.

11

☆の線から、上を斜めに折る。

Fold diagonally from the ☆ line .

12

両側ともあいだを開いて耳をつくる。

Open both sides to make ears.

13

口のところから空気を入れて、ふくらませて、できあがり。

Add air from the rabbit's mouth to puff out. Finished!

雪ん子 Yukinko [see page 63]

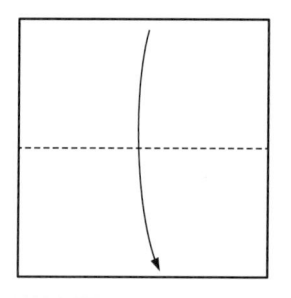

1
半分に折る。
Fold in half.

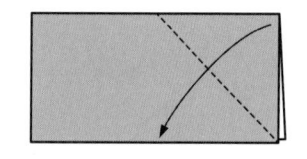

2
図の位置で折る。
Fold as shown.

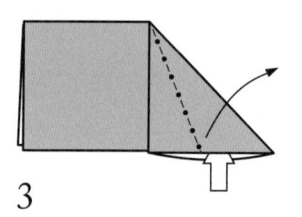

3
中を開きながら折る。
Open and squash.

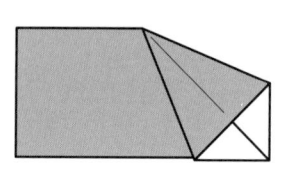

4
折ったところ。
Make this shape.

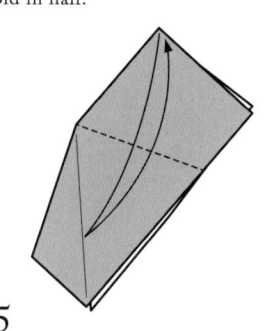

5
図の位置で折りすじつける。
Make a crease as shown.

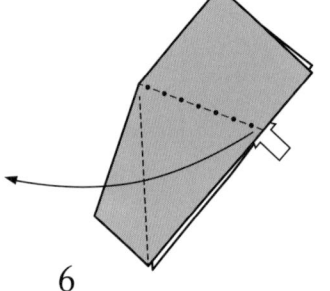

6
中を開きながら折る。
Open and fold down.

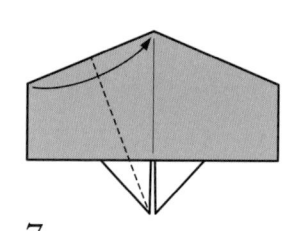

7
かどとかどが合うように折る。
Fold the corners together.

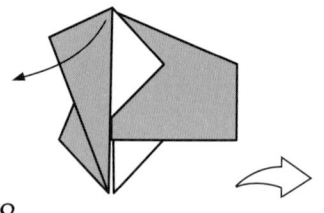

8
7の形に戻す。右側も同様にする。
Return to the shape of step7.
Repeat on the right side.

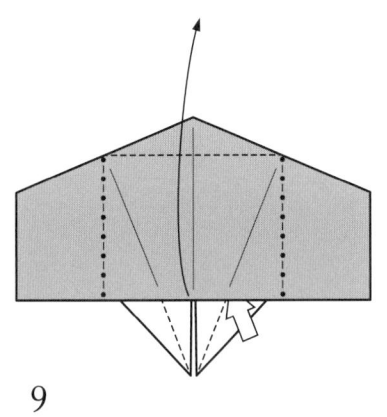

9

折りすじをつけて、あいだを開いて上の
紙をたたみながら折る。

Make creases and fold the top flap up.

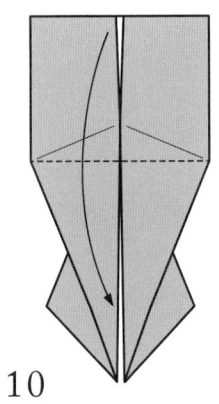

10

図の位置で折る。

Fold as shown.

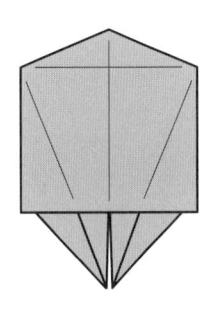

11

折ったところ。

Make this shape.

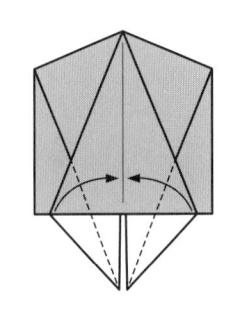

12

まん中に合うように折る。

Fold as shown.

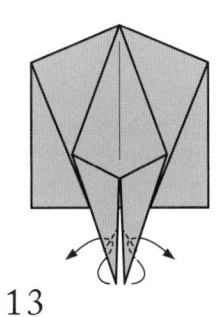

13

中わり折り（P.15）する。

Inside reverse fold (page15).

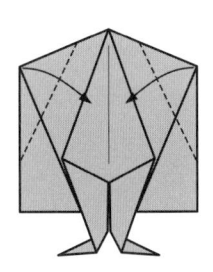

14

図の位置で折る。

Fold as shown.

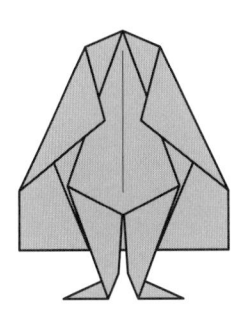

できあがり
Finished!

監修——小林一夫 こばやし・かずお

1941年東京生まれ。お茶の水 おりがみ会館館長。内閣府認証NPO法人国際おりがみ協会理事長。全国の折り紙教室で指導や講演を行うかたわら、世界各国で折り紙や和紙を通じた国際交流、日本文化の紹介活動を行なっている。折り紙に関する著書多数。

Editorial Supervisor —— Kazuo Kobayashi

Born in Tokyo in 1941, Kazuo Kobayashi is the Director of the Ochanomizu Origami Kaikan and the president of the International Origami Association, a registered NPO. He teaches classes and lectures about origami all over Japan, while also organizing programs that use *washi* paper and origami to foster international exchange and introduce Japanese culture to the world. He has published many books about origami.

編集——宮下 真（オフィスM2）
アートディレクション——有山達也
デザイン——山本祐衣（アリヤマデザインストア）
撮影——野村知也
作品制作・折り図協力——渡部浩美
英訳—— Sarah McNally
校正——村上理恵、堀ゆみ子
折り図トレース・DTP——田村浩子（株式会社ウエイド 手芸制作部）

千代紙・撮影協力——株式会社ゆしまの小林
　　　　　　　　　　お茶の水 おりがみ会館
　　　　　　　　　　URL https://www.origamikaikan.co.jp/

参考文献————『日本の文様』（小林一夫著・日本ヴォーグ社）
　　　　　　　『日本・中国の文様事典』（視覚デザイン研究所）

英訳付き 日本折り紙帖

監修者　小林一夫
発行者　池田士文
印刷所　TOPPANクロレ株式会社
製本所　TOPPANクロレ株式会社
発行所　株式会社池田書店
　　　　東京都新宿区弁天町43番地（〒162-0851）
　　　　☎ 03-3267-6821（代）／振替 00120-9-60072
　　　　落丁・乱丁はおとりかえいたします。

©K. K. Ikeda Shoten 2019, Printed in Japan
ISBN978-4-262-15295-0

25039507